Psalms *to* Soothe *a* Woman's heart

PRESENTED TO

PRESENTED BY

DATE

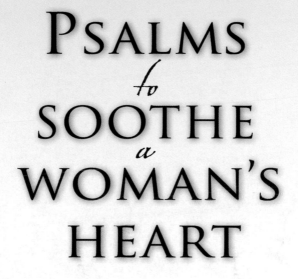

Psalms *to* SOOTHE *a* WOMAN'S HEART

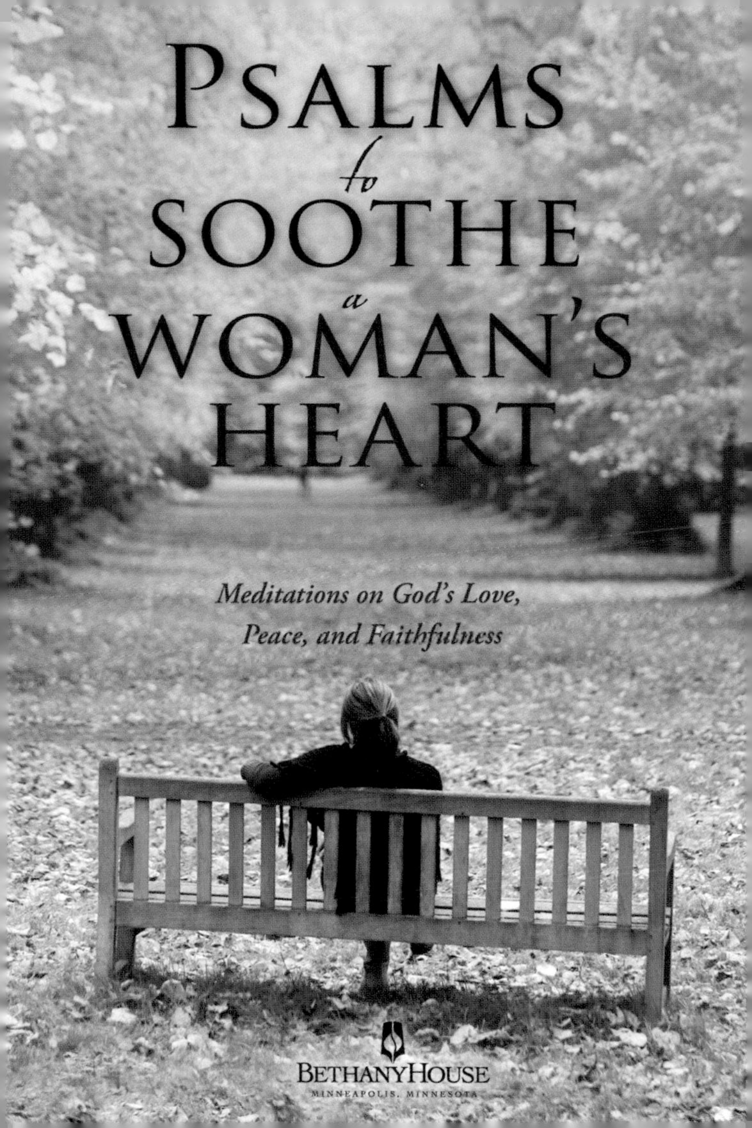

Psalms to SOOTHE a WOMAN'S HEART

Meditations on God's Love, Peace, and Faithfulness

BETHANY HOUSE

MINNEAPOLIS, MINNESOTA

Psalms to Soothe a Woman's Heart

Copyright © 2009 by GRQ, Inc.

Published by Bethany House Publishers
11400 Hampshire Avenue South
Bloomington, Minnesota 55438

Bethany House Publishers is a division of Baker Publishing Group, Grand Rapids, Michigan.

Scripture quotations noted AMP are from *The Amplified Bible, Old Testament*. Copyright © 1965, 1987 by The Zondervan Corporation. *The Amplified New Testament*. Copyright © 1954, 1958, 1987 by The Lockman Foundation. Used by permission.

Scripture quotations noted CEV are taken from *THE CONTEMPORARY ENGLISH VERSION*. Copyright © 1991 by the American Bible Society. Used by permission.

Scripture quotations noted ESV are from *The Holy Bible, English Standard Version,* copyright © 2001 by Crossway Bibles, a division of Good News Publishers. Used by permission. All rights reserved.

Scripture quotations noted GOD'S WORD are from *God's Word,* a copyrighted work of God's Word to the Nations Bible Society. Copyright © 1995 by God's Word to the Nations Bible Society. Used by permission. All rights reserved.

Scripture quotations noted GNT are from the *Good News Translation,* Second Edition, copyright © 1992 by American Bible Society. Used by permission. All rights reserved.

Scripture quotations noted HCSB have been taken from the *Holman Christian Standard Bible®,* copyright © 1999, 2000, 2002, 2003 by Holman Bible Publishers. Used by permission. Holman Christian Standard Bible®, Holman CSB® and HCSB® are federally registered trademarks of Holman Bible Publishers.

Scripture quotations noted MSG are taken from *THE MESSAGE: The New Testament, Psalms and Proverbs*. Copyright © 1993, 1994, 1995 by Eugene H. Peterson. All rights reserved.

Scripture quotations noted NASB are taken from the *NEW AMERICAN STANDARD BIBLE®*. Copyright © 1960, 1962, 1963–1968, 1971, 1973–1975, 1977, 1995 by the Lockman Foundation. Used by permission.

Scripture quotations noted NCV are from *The Holy Bible, New Century Version,* copyright © 1987, 1988, 1991 by Word Publishing, a division of Thomas Nelson, Inc. All rights reserved. Used by permission.

Scripture quotations noted NIV are taken from the *Holy Bible: New International Version* (North American Edition) ® Copyright © 1973–1978, 1984, by the International Bible Society. Used by permission of Zondervan. All rights reserved.

Scripture quotations noted NKJV are taken from *THE NEW KING JAMES VERSION*. Copyright © 1979, 1980, 1982, Thomas Nelson, Inc., Publishers.

Scripture quotations noted NLT are taken from the *Holy Bible, New Living Translation,* copyright © 1996. Used by permission of Tyndale House Publishers, Inc., Wheaton, Illinois 60189. All rights reserved.

All rights reserved. No part of this publication may be reproduced, stored in a retrieval system, or transmitted in any form or by any means—electronic, mechanical, photocopying, recording, or any other—without the prior written permission of the publisher. The only exception is brief quotations in printed reviews.

ISBN: 978-0-7642-0551-4

Editor: Lila Empson
Associate Editor: Natasha Sperling
Writer: Jennifer B. Rosania
Design: Whisner Design Group

Printed in China. All rights reserved under International Copyright Law. Contents and/or cover may not be reproduced in whole or in part in any form without the express written consent of the publisher.

09 10 11 4 3 2 1

Oh, the joys of those who . . .
delight in the law of the LORD,
meditating on it day and night. . . .
They prosper in all they do.

PSALM 1:1–3 NLT

CONTENTS

INTRODUCTION

Throughout the ages the book of Psalms has been an inspiration to countless people. Not only does it hold some of the most beautiful verses ever written about the joys and sorrows of the human heart, but it also brings you to the very throne of heaven as it describes your loving God.

Originally a worship book for the people of Israel, the Psalms were compiled during a time period of more than a thousand years—from the time of the Exodus from Egypt until after the Babylonian captivity. Seventy-three of the psalms were composed by King David; however, Moses, Solomon, Asaph, and possibly King Hezekiah also contributed to this exquisite book of hymns, prayers, and poetry. Their insights are recorded to encourage you and bring you closer to God.

Psalms to Soothe a Woman's Heart was written with you in mind. It connects the daily struggles you face with the profound wisdom of the Bible. Looking for peace in the Psalms is not a random choice on your part. You are looking in the only place where you can find peace: in God. Through the Psalms you will discover the intimate relationship God wants to have with you—how he can be your Defender, Provider, Healer, and King no matter what you face.

Friend, God is waiting to fill you with joy and to comfort you with his presence each day. Read the inspirational verses, pray, worship God, and enjoy your journey through the Psalms. May your time with God completely bless your soul.

When I am hurting, I find comfort
in your promise that leads to life.

PSALM 119:50 CEV

Always

I keep the LORD in mind always.
Because He is at my right hand,
I will not be shaken.

PSALM 16:8 HCSB

TO BE BLESSED

*Happy are those who . . . love the LORD's teachings,
and they think about those teachings day and night.*
PSALM 1:1–2 NCV

When you have a wounded heart, you may find it difficult to know where to turn. You look outwardly to loved

ones and those who purport to know
the answers to your hurt, but there is
no real comfort. You look into yourself and find pain and confusion
there. Where can you go to soothe
your soul?

Friend, it is no coincidence that your
search has brought you to the Psalms. It is not in looking out or in, but *up* to God that that you will find what
you are seeking. God promises you blessing when you
read and embrace the Bible; God promises that you will
be filled with love, joy, purpose, and peace. Isn't that what
your heart has been aching for, after all?

*God, I need you. Thank you for revealing yourself to
me through the Psalms and for healing my
heart. Only you can truly bless me. Amen.*

They are strong, like a tree planted by a river.
The tree produces fruit in season, and its leaves
don't die. Everything they do will succeed.

PSALM 1:3 NCV

TIME IN HIS PRESENCE

*Blessed (happy, fortunate, and to be envied) are all
those who seek refuge and put their trust in Him!*
PSALM 2:12 AMP

Knowing God is a privilege. Although some have the
good fortune of meeting with presidents and prime min-
isters, few are invited into their inner sanctuary—and no

one is eternally changed by the
encounter.

Yet God invites you to know him
in the most profound way possible
and to embrace his best for your
life. The Creator of the universe
beckons you to be transformed by
his divine mercy, wisdom, and
provision, and to know the unlimited power and love that
have been made available to you.

Spending time in God's presence is a precious gift—one
that you have been given to enjoy at any moment, no matter the hour or the reason. Therefore, do not decline his
invitation. It is the best appointment you will keep all day.

*God, thank you so much for inviting me into your
presence, transforming my life, and loving me. I praise
and worship you with all of my heart. Amen.*

Worship God in adoring embrace,
celebrate in trembling awe.

PSALM 2:11 MSG

A SURE DEFENDER

*With my voice I cry to the Lord, and He hears
and answers me out of His holy hill.*

PSALM 3:4 AMP

As King David considered his options, he realized that there could be no good resolution to the conflict. His son Absalom had rallied forces to take the throne of Israel

away from him. It was an impossible situation—either David would lose his kingdom and life or he would lose his son. No matter the outcome, his heart and his nation would be broken. Psalm 3 is the prayer that flowed from the anguish within him.

Are you facing a situation that seems completely hopeless? Go to God. Even if you cannot see a constructive way out, he can, and he knows exactly what is best for everyone involved. Therefore, trust him. He is your Shield and Defender, and if you obey him, he will surely lead you to triumph.

*God, thank you for not only hearing me but also for
understanding my situation better than I do. I will trust
you to guide me to the best solution. Amen.*

You are my shield, and you give
me victory and great honor.

PSALM 3:3 CEV

TRUE HEALING

*O God of my righteousness! You have given
me relief when I was in distress.*

PSALM 4:1 ESV

Whether it is pain or paralysis in your limbs or an illness
that affects you internally, health problems can severely
limit what you can accomplish. The same is true for

emotional and spiritual difficulties. Fears and regrets can tor-
ment you to the point that you
feel trapped in your situation.

In your own power, you can do
nothing to set yourself free, yet
God can overcome whatever you
are facing. In fact, God will work through your affliction
to make you genuinely complete and help you fulfill your
purpose in life.

Therefore, trust him to heal you to the depths of your
soul. He will turn your limitations into opportunities for
surprising fruitfulness and teach you how to live in his
comfort and abundance.

*God, thank you for truly healing my distress and giving
relief to my troubled soul. I trust you to turn this place
of pain into a reason for praising you. Amen.*

You have given me greater joy than those who have abundant harvests of grain and new wine.

PSALM 4:7 NLT

A MANTLE OF LOVE

*Let all those who take refuge and put their trust in You
rejoice; let them ever sing and shout for joy, because
You make a covering over them and defend them.*

PSALM 5:11 AMP

It has been speculated that intelligent women prefer to be
perceived as physically attractive and that good-looking

women wish to be seen as clever. Yet
what most women truly desire is to be
accepted. Adored. Cherished. Loved.

That's exactly what you are when you
take refuge in God. As you spend time
with Him, He envelops you in His
majesty and grace, and His splendor
shines through you. You become not

only pretty, but beautiful; not just smart, but wise. Not
only accepted, adored, cherished, and loved—but merciful, gentle, joyful, and loving.

Therefore, instead of worrying about whether you are
smart or pretty, rejoice that you're clothed in God's mantle of love. Because that, friend, is what makes you truly
exceptional.

*God, thank you for covering me with the mantle of your
love. Your presence makes me beautiful and wise,
and I praise you with all my heart. Amen.*

*You bless the godly, O L*ORD*; you surround*
them with your shield of love.

PSALM 5:12 NLT

HE HEARS

The Lord has heard the voice of my weeping. The Lord has heard my supplication; the Lord will receive my prayer.

PSALM 6:8–9 NKJV

At times you may confide in people, and although they appear to be paying attention, they may not really grasp

what you're telling them. They do not comprehend the depth of your emotions or the helplessness of your situation. Even if they can empathize with you, they will be unable to offer you genuine, lasting relief.

Yet when you call out to God, he truly hears you—even the words you don't say. He understands the pain you feel and is committed to giving you the most effective help with whatever you're facing.

Have you taken your troubles to others, only to be let down? Then turn your concerns over to God. He's always glad to listen and has promised never to fail you. Trust him.

God, thank you for hearing my prayers—even the wordless ones that come from my heart. Truly, you are my most wonderful confidant, and I praise you. Amen.

*O L*ORD*, rescue my soul; save me*
because of Your lovingkindness.

PSALM **6:4** NASB

WAITING FOR JUSTICE

Judge me and show that I am honest and innocent. You know every heart and mind, and you always do right.

PSALM 7:8–9 CEV

It can be truly disheartening when others advance because of the lies they have told about you. That is what happened

to David. Those who were jealous of his success accused him of treason. With his life in danger and no way to defend himself, David turned to the only One he could truly count on: God. David was confident that the Lord would defend him and prove his innocence.

Are you powerless to counteract the false charges of others? Are their allegations endangering your future? Do not fear. Just as God defended David, he will protect you as well. Therefore, continue to honor God in every aspect of your life, and be patient. His justice is coming, and soon everyone will know the truth.

God, thank you for seeing my innocence and for defending me. However long it takes, I trust you to bring justice out of this situation. Amen.

*You, God, are my shield, the protector
of everyone whose heart is right.*

PSALM 7:10 CEV

WHY SHOULD HE CARE?

*When I look at the night sky and see the work of your
fingers—the moon and the stars you set in place—what
are . . . human beings that you should care for them?*
PSALM 8:3–4 NLT

Sometimes it is surprising to discover how deeply and sincerely you are loved. Perhaps you even find others' devotion

difficult to accept because you are
accustomed to thinking of yourself as
unlovable or unworthy.

This may be especially true when considering God's perfect, unconditional
love. After all, he is majestic and
holy—capable of creating the world
and everything in it. Surely there are

better, more worthy creatures to love, right? Not to God.

God's nature is love, and he created you for the glorious
purpose of expressing his wonderful, unlimited care for
you. Therefore, accept it! Because there is nothing you
could ever do to make him stop loving you.

*My God, thank you so much for loving me unconditionally!
Help me to accept the reality of your love with all
my heart, soul, mind, and strength. Amen.*

*O LORD, our Lord, how majestic is Your name
in all the earth, who have displayed Your
splendor above the heavens!*

PSALM 8:1 NASB

A WELCOME PURSUIT

Those who know your name will trust in you, for
you, LORD, have never forsaken those who seek you.
PSALM 9:10 NIV

Chase fame, power, accomplishments, or social status,
and you may discover that the more you have, the more

unstable you feel. Try to fill your
innermost needs with wealth, relationships, or activities, and you will
probably find yourself with a
greater sense of dissatisfaction than
you have ever felt before. Attempt
to escape your sorrows with food,
alcohol, or other substances, and
the gnawing emptiness within you will only increase.

Yet pursue God, and the doors of joy and fulfillment will
spring open. Not only does he give you a firm place to
stand and satisfy your soul, but he also fills your life with
his presence, love, and purpose. Seek him with all of your
heart, therefore, because you will certainly find what you
are looking for.

God, I want to know you more—teach me your ways.
Thank you that when I seek you, I find everything
I need and all that my heart desires. Amen.

The LORD has made Himself known.

PSALM 9:16 NASB

DECEPTIVE FEELINGS

O LORD, why do you stand so far away?
Why do you hide when I am in trouble?
PSALM 10:1 NLT

The circumstances that trouble you may suggest that God has abandoned you. Yet the truth is, he will never

leave you or forsake you. It may seem as if God is ignoring your prayers and tears, but he takes special care of each one. Your heart may even cry out, "My God, why don't you help me?" However, he is working all things out for your good even when you cannot see it.

At times your feelings will tempt you to doubt God, which is why you must always cling to the promises he gives you in his Word. Never allow your emotions to cloud the truth of God's unfailing love. The fact is, he is with you and will never fail you. Therefore, rejoice in his holy name.

God, I praise you for sticking by me—even when my heart begins to wander. Please forgive me for doubting you. Help me to trust you more. Amen.

Lord, surely you see these cruel and evil things.
People in trouble look to you for help. You
are the one who helps the orphans.

PSALM 10:14 NCV

A HEAVENLY PERSPECTIVE

The LORD is in his holy temple; the LORD is on his heavenly throne. He observes the sons of men; his eyes examine them.
PSALM 11:4 NIV

Is safety important to you? Would you like to feel secure in your home, finances, relationships, and occupation? Are you ever afraid of the future—of being unprepared for the

challenges ahead?

Fears about the unknown can steal your peace. Yet understand that although your perspective is limited, God's is not. That is why your best safeguard is always to trust him.

God sees the troubles on the path before you, and he can lead you through them unharmed. He also examines the dangers within you and frees you from them.

Therefore, be confident in God's unfailing perspective and discover real security in your relationship with him.

God, you know my fears and my need for security.
Help me to trust and obey you so that I can remain
in the center of your perfect care. Amen.

I trust in the LORD for protection.

PSALM 11:1 NCV

THE COMING RESCUE

"Because of the oppression of the weak and the groaning of the needy, I will now arise," says the LORD. "I will protect them from those who malign them."

PSALM 12:5 NIV

When David faced Goliath, he was merely a boy and was unfamiliar with the sword. One might imagine that David was afraid to face the massive giant. After all, everyone else in Israel was. Yet instead of being frightened by Goliath's threats, David remembered the faithfulness of God, and he trusted the Lord to rescue him.

Are you on your own to face a challenge that is too enormous to handle? Call out to God, and obey whatever he tells you. Just as he rescued David by empowering him to slay Goliath, he will give you triumph over your trial if you will trust him. So do not fear. Your deliverance is coming. Watch for it.

God, no challenge is too difficult for you! Thank you for giving me hope in this trial. I know I am never alone or defeated as long as you're with me. Amen.

The words of the LORD are pure words,
like silver tried in a furnace of earth,
purified seven times.

PSALM 12:6 NKJV

INTERMINABLE?

How long, O LORD? Will you forget me forever? . . .
Consider and answer me, O LORD my God.
PSALM 13:1, 3 ESV

After weeks, months, perhaps even years of waiting for the Lord to work in a certain situation, you may feel weary and your hope may be fading. Maybe you are

wondering, *Why is God taking so long? Why isn't he answering my prayers? Will this ever end?*

Waiting is difficult, but it is also necessary because it builds your faith in him. That is because you resolve to trust him even when

every circumstance tells you not to. God rewards you by fulfilling the desires of your heart in a way more wonderful than you ever thought possible.

Therefore, friend, do not be discouraged—your wait is not in vain. God's provision is coming, and when it does, you will truly have great reason to rejoice.

God, thank you for this encouragement—I know you
have not forgotten me. Help me to wait patiently and
expectantly for your answer to my prayers. Amen.

I've thrown myself headlong into your arms—I'm celebrating your rescue. I'm singing at the top of my lungs, I'm so full of answered prayers.

PSALM 13:5–6 MSG

NOT NATURAL ... SUPERNATURAL

There is no one who does good.
PSALM 14:1 NASB

Have you ever wondered if something within you fights against honoring God? If so, you are right. It is contrary to human nature to submit to him. People's natural incli-

nations can only lead to destruction; there is nothing inherently good about them.

When you begin to seek God, it is not by natural means; rather, he draws you *supernaturally* by his Spirit. In fact, when you believe in him to save you, he gives you his

Holy Spirit to guide, teach, and transform you. It is then that you can obey him, that you can truly do good.

Through the power of God's Spirit, you can choose to honor him. Therefore, embrace the supernatural life and enjoy his extraordinary blessings. Because what he offers you is truly out of this world.

God, thank you for drawing me to you by your Spirit.
Teach me the difference between your direction and my
natural desires so I can always honor you. Amen.

From heaven the LORD looks down to see if anyone is wise enough to search for him.

PSALM 14:2 CEV

Hope

*Show me your ways, O L*ORD*, teach me your paths;*
guide me in your truth and teach me, for you are
God my Savior, and my hope is in you all day long.

PSALM 25:4–5 NIV

AM I GOOD ENOUGH?

> LORD, *who can dwell in Your tent?*
> *Who can live on Your holy mountain?*
> PSALM 15:1 HCSB

Psalm 15 goes to the heart of humanity's deepest problem—is anyone worthy of living in heaven with God?

You are told that you must be honest and kind and that you must keep all the Lord's commands and never do wrong to others. Reviewing these requirements, you may question whether you can ever truly meet God's standards.

That is as it should be. The inability to be *good enough* makes you aware of your need for God's help, which he graciously provided through the death and resurrection of his Son, Jesus Christ.

When you trust him for salvation, God covers you with his righteousness and makes you worthy of dwelling with God for eternity. So believe in him, trusting his provision. Because then you can rest in *his* goodness forever.

God, I know I cannot make myself worthy of heaven, so I
trust you for salvation. Thank you for forgiving my sins
and covering me with your goodness. Amen.

Such people will stand firm forever.

PSALM 15:5 NLT

GOOD BOUNDARIES

*LORD, you have assigned me my portion and my
cup; you have made my lot secure. The boundary
lines have fallen for me in pleasant places.*

PSALM 16:5–6 NIV

God created you at this appointed time in history and in
your unique circumstances for a reason. Your experiences

have not only shaped your per-
sonality and values, but they will
affect how you serve God and to
whom you are able to minister.

Although your life may be difficult at present, it is not a mistake
that you are where you are. God
has set the boundaries of your life not for harm, but for
good. Not to cause you pain, but to give you purpose.

You may not understand how God could use your situation, but he will bless you abundantly if you will allow
him to lead you. Therefore, listen to him and seek his
wisdom in your circumstances. Then rejoice as he turns
your limitations into wonderful opportunities.

*God, I praise you for working all things out for my good.
Thank you for using my life's boundaries for your glory,
the benefit of others, and my edification. Amen.*

I will praise the LORD who counsels me—even at night my conscience instructs me. I keep the LORD in mind always. Because He is at my right hand, I will not be shaken.

PSALM 16:7–8 HCSB

ALWAYS WITH YOU

*I feel completely secure, because you protect me from
the power of death. I have served you faithfully,
and you will not abandon me.*

PSALM 16:9–10 GNT

Loneliness can strike for many reasons: loss, rejection,
and separation from loved ones. Yet if you allow it to

consume you, alienation, insecurity,
and thoughts of unworthiness can
become your private prison, one that
is incredibly destructive and difficult
to escape from.

Friend, God wants to free you from
your loneliness through his enduring
presence and healing care. With him,
you never have to fear being alone, because he assures
you of his unfailing love. As you grow closer to him, he
not only teaches you to have a fulfilling relationship with
himself, but with others as well.

Whenever the bondage of loneliness begins to close
around your heart, trust the One who will never leave you.

*God, I thank you for never leaving or forsaking me.
Thank you for freeing me from the bondage of loneliness
and teaching me to love others as you do. Amen.*

You will show me the path that leads to life;
your presence fills me with joy and
brings me pleasure forever.

PSALM 16:11 GNT

SWEET VINDICATION

*Show Your marvelous lovingkindness by Your
right hand, O You who save those who trust in
You from those who rise up against them.*

Psalm 17:7 NKJV

Whenever you serve God, there will be those who do not
understand your devotion to him and may even oppose

what he has commanded you to
do. Their heated words and antag-
onism may be discouraging, but be
strong. Continue to do what is
right—honoring the Lord.

As hard as they try, no one can
prevent God from fulfilling his
purpose for you. In addition, when you honor him faithfully, his loving character will shine through you.

Therefore, instead of growing angry with your adversaries,
pray that they will accept the freedom that God offers.
Then, whether or not they decide to follow him, you will
have succeeded in doing what is right and keeping your
heart clean. That is all the vindication you really need.

*God, I do pray for those who oppose your work in the
world. Help them to accept the truth of your love and
help me to always honor you. Amen.*

You have tested my heart; You have visited by night; You have tried me and found nothing [evil].

PSALM 17:3 HCSB

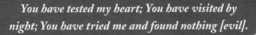

WHEN YOU PRAY

My cry to him reached his ears. Then the earth reeled and rocked; the foundations also of the mountains trembled and quaked.

PSALM 18:6–7 ESV

David was thankful. As he recalled the many times God had delivered him from dangerous foes, he could not help

but testify about the Lord's unfailing faithfulness. Whatever the situation, no matter how dire the trial, God *always* answered his prayers.

However, you may wonder what happens when *you* pray. Does God respond to you as he did David?

Yes, he does. He moves heaven and earth to answer anyone who calls to him with faith and sincerity. Although his reply may not be what you expect, he never fails to do what is in your best interest.

Therefore, call out to the Lord with whatever concerns you. David found him exceedingly faithful, and there is no doubt you will too.

God, thank you for hearing my prayers and for answering me as you did King David. Truly, you are faithful, loving, and worthy of all my praise. Amen.

He brought me out to a wide-open place;
He rescued me because He delighted in me.

PSALM 18:19 HCSB

THE BUILDER OF GREATNESS

Your gentleness has made me great.

PSALM 18:35 NKJV

God uses each challenge you experience to mold you into a person of significance and excellence. This does not imply he is making you wealthy or famous by the  world's standards; rather, it means he is preparing you to reveal his glory.

Perhaps this seems unlikely to you. Maybe you once thought yourself special, but the years have destroyed the dreams that once thrilled your heart. Yet just as God took the shepherd David and made him a king, he can lift you out of your ordinary situation and reveal your wonderful potential, if you will let him.

Will you accept the trials that come as his training and allow him to build greatness in you? It is your choice. So embrace the future that is better than you can imagine.

God, thank you for seeing more in me than I see in myself. I trust you to use every situation to develop your godly excellence in me. To you be all the glory. Amen.

LORD, You light my lamp; my God illuminates my darkness. With You I can attack a barrier, and with my God I can leap over a wall.

PSALM 18:28–29 HCSB

A STORY TO TELL

*The heavens declare the glory of God,
and the sky above proclaims his handiwork.*

PSALM 19:1 ESV

All the wonders of the heavens declare the glory of God and proclaim his exquisite handiwork. And guess what?

You do too.

When you believe in God, you become a living psalm, a walking demonstration that he exists, he is faithful, and he does all things well. People will experience his presence through the words you speak, your attitude, and even your actions toward them. They will realize that the God of grace loves them and wants to illuminate their life with his joy, mercy, and salvation.

Is that what you are saying with your life? Are you shining brightly as a light to those who need God's hope? You have a story to tell, so do it well. It may make an eternal difference to those who hear you.

God, I am so inspired to tell others your story. Guide my words and my heart so that I can honor you and encourage others to know you as well. Amen.

Let the words of my mouth and the meditation of my heart be acceptable in Your sight, O L ORD, my strength and my Redeemer.

PSALM 19:14 NKJV

LOVE FOR HIS WORD

The precepts of the LORD are right,
giving joy to the heart.
PSALM 19:8 NIV

Of all the books in the world, none has endured as well or changed as many lives as the Bible. That is because it

is God's unique revelation of himself. Through his Word and his Spirit within you, you get to know your Creator, you are able to receive his comfort and direction, and you discover how to live a life that is pleasing to him.

Are you reading the psalms as you are reading this devotional? Are they blessing your heart and illuminating your soul? God wants to give you joy through this wonderful love letter he has inspired for your edification. Therefore, embrace this treasure trove of wisdom and allow him to change your life through it. Certainly it is the best book you will ever read.

God, I praise you for your wonderful Word. Create a love
for your precepts and promises in me and help me to
know you better through it. Amen.

The judgments of the Lord are true; they are completely right. They are worth more than gold, even the purest gold. They are sweeter than honey, even the finest honey. By them your servant is warned. Keeping them brings great reward.

PSALM 19:9–11 NCV

A REASON FOR CONFIDENCE

*May he give you what you desire and
make all your plans succeed.*
PSALM 20:4 GNT

Throughout the Bible, you read of people who had
amazing challenges but were able to face them with

astonishing confidence and
assurance. Moses, Joshua,
David, Paul—all faced terrible
odds but did not falter. How
was it possible?

The answer is not found in
their strength, but in the might
of the One they believed in wholeheartedly. They all
trusted God and realized that no matter how bad the situation, he could overcome it.

You should have confidence for the same reason. No
matter what God calls you to do, you will see the victory
and the wonderful blessings he has for you as long as you
obey him. You may not have great earthly resources, but
you have God, and he makes you a winner every time.

*God, thank you for giving me such a wonderful reason
for confidence! Help me to trust you wholeheartedly
and obey you always. Amen.*

Some trust in their war chariots and others in their horses, but we trust in the power of the LORD our God. Such people will stumble and fall, but we will rise and stand firm.

PSALM 20:7–8 GNT

OF PRAISE AND POWER

Be exalted, Lord, in Your strength;
we will sing and praise Your power.
PSALM 21:13 AMP

Allow the words to roll from your lips, "Lord, I praise your wonderful power." Say the phrase aloud, "My God, I trust your faultless strength."

Is this exercise of adoration difficult for you today? Is there an issue weighing on your heart that prevents you from adoring the Lord? If so, it is even more essential for you to turn your thoughts away from your suffering and to his sufficiency, to replace the pain of your trials with the reality of his triumph.

Worship the Lord who can and will help you. Rejoice and be glad that he is with you and will never fail. It is when you refocus your attention on him that you will see victory as a possibility. That, friend, is the true power of praise.

God, I want to trust you—so I will praise you with an
open heart. I rejoice in your faultless strength and know
your mighty hand will provide the victory. Amen.

*You have granted him the desire of his heart
and have not withheld the request of his lips.
You welcomed him with rich blessings.*

PSALM 21:2–3 NIV

A RECORD OF RESCUE

Our ancestors trusted you. They trusted, and you rescued them. They cried to you and were saved. They trusted you and were never disappointed.
PSALM 22:4–5 GOD'S WORD

Hundreds of prophecies throughout the Old Testament predicted the coming of the One who would deliver peo-

ple from their sins. Psalm 22 contains some of the particulars about the Messiah, and almost a thousand years after it was written those details came true in the person of Jesus Christ.

Jesus is living proof that the Lord keeps all of his promises. Psalm 22 is a reminder that all who trust in

him are never disappointed.

Therefore, trust the Lord Jesus to save you from your sins and to rescue you in all of your difficult circumstances. You can count on him, because not only is his record the best—it is perfect.

God, you are utterly astounding! Thank you for saving me from my sins and rescuing me from my troubles. Truly you are worthy of all my praise! Amen.

In the midst of the assembly I will praise You.
*You who fear the L*ORD*, praise Him!*

PSALM 22:22–23 NKJV

THE SHEPHERD'S REPUTATION

*He renews my soul. He guides me along the paths
of righteousness for the sake of his name.*
PSALM 23:3 GOD'S WORD

One can generally deduce the skill of the shepherd by the
condition of his sheep. Is the flock cared for? Healthy,

well-fed, free of parasites and injuries?
This is due to the shepherd's watchful
leadership. He nurtures his lambs with
skill and understanding and gladly gives
his life to rescue them from danger.

The same is true for your shepherd—
the Lord God. He nourishes your soul
through his Word and Spirit. He pro-
tects you from paths that would destroy you, and exercises
your faith so you can grow strong and healthy. He guides
you through the perils of life to places of peace.

How well you are cared for reflects on his name, so he is
not going to let you down. Therefore, trust the Shepherd.
With him, you shall surely never want.

*Lord, you are my wonderful shepherd. Thank you for
leading me so faithfully. May my life bring praise to your
good, holy, and merciful name. Amen.*

The L ORD is my shepherd; I have everything I need. . . . I know that your goodness and love will be with me all my life; and your house will be my home as long as I live.

PSALM 23:1, 6 GNT

THE GOD YOU LOVE

Who is this great king? He is the LORD, strong and mighty, the LORD, victorious in battle.
PSALM 24:8 GNT

Do you love God for what he does or because of who he is? Do you pay him lip service to get what you want, or

do you worship him because you are truly in awe of his amazing grace?

Like you, God desires to be loved for himself—for you to honor him because he is astoundingly imaginative, unwaveringly kind, steadfastly holy, completely powerful, and absolutely wise. He also wants to have a deep, abiding relationship with you so you can experience his unconditional love.

So consider: Why do you seek him? Are you looking for someone to cater to your needs? Or have you realized that you are simply not whole without him in your life? Do you praise him for your sake or for his?

God, I want to love you for who you are—even though my motivation is sometimes misplaced. Help me to know you and love you more every day. Amen.

The earth is the LORD's, and all it contains,
the world, and those who dwell in it.

PSALM 24:1 NASB

WHAT DO I DO?

Make Your ways known to me, LORD; teach me Your paths. Guide me in Your truth and teach me, for You are the God of my salvation; I wait for You all day long.
PSALM 25:4–5 HCSB

"I don't know what to do." This is difficult to admit if you are accustomed to being self-sufficient and finding your  own way in every situation. When this realization settles in, the anxiety may overwhelm you, especially if others are depending upon you to do what is best. With all options exhausted, where can you turn?

These circumstances did not happen by chance. God will allow you to reach the end of your resources so you will turn to him and seek his guidance.

Friend, stop being so self-reliant. Instead of trying to figure out what to do or thinking that you must have all the answers, pray to him. Read the Bible. Listen for his direction. He *does* know what to do, and he will certainly show you the very best path to take.

God, it is so hard to give up control. Please forgive me for being so resistant to your direction. Thank you for your gentleness and for helping me through this trial. Amen.

Those who respect the Lord? He will point them to the best way. . . . My eyes are always looking to the Lord for help. He will keep me from any traps.

PSALM 25:12, 15 NCV

Wonderful

You, LORD God, have done many wonderful things, and you have planned marvelous things for us. No one is like you! I would never be able to tell all you have done.

PSALM 40:5 CEV

STABILITY

*Now I stand on solid ground,
and I will publicly praise the LORD.*
PSALM 26:12 NLT

Where do you go for stability? When your world crumbles around you, where do you turn? Friend, God should

not be your last resort.

Because when chaotic situations occur, only he can steady you with his assurance, teach you wisdom and self-control, and train you to remain faithful. Rather than allowing events to throw you off balance, he shows you how to stay in the center of his will and cling to his unwavering promises.

God is the only One who can truly bring you stability because he is completely consistent and unchanging—he stays steady, though the rest of the world may tremble. Therefore, stand on solid ground by setting your feet on the path God has for you. There, you will surely never be shaken.

God, what would I do without you to cling to? I praise you for your faultless character that I can always depend upon. Truly you are wonderful. Amen.

Your steadfast love is before my eyes,
and I walk in your faithfulness.

PSALM 26:3 ESV

NEVER DESPAIR

*I would have despaired unless I had believed that I would see
the goodness of the LORD in the land of the living.*

PSALM 27:13 NASB

Despair can drive you to all sorts of destructive behaviors.
You become so anxious to see your desires fulfilled that you

turn to options that oppose God's
best for you. You may even convince
yourself that he has abandoned you.

Of course, that is untrue. God *will*
help you, in his timing. Yet that is
why you need to protect yourself
from despair while you are waiting
for him to work—so you do not

miss his perfect will for you.

Therefore, meditate daily on his Word, on his promises,
and on the occasions he has rescued you, because then it is
so much easier to hold on to your hope. Wait expectantly
for God's goodness no matter how long it takes, because
that is the perfect position to be in to receive his very best.

*God, thank you for rescuing me when I have come so close
to despair. Help me to stay steadfast in hope and to
always trust your perfect will. Amen.*

*Wait on the LORD; be of good courage, and He shall
strengthen your heart; wait, I say, on the LORD!*

PSALM 27:14 NKJV

THE SILENT TREATMENT

*O Lord my Rock, be not deaf and silent to me. . . . Hear
the voice of my supplication as I cry to You for help.*

PSALM 28:1–2 AMP

You need answers, so you humble yourself before God's
throne and listen. However, there is no response. There
is not even the hint of a reply.

There is only silence.

Repeatedly you pray, wondering
why he has not addressed your
pleas, searching your soul to see if
you have done anything wrong.
Your ears strain for a word. Soon
your quest is no longer about get-
ting an answer. You just want to hear his voice. Friend,
that is exactly where you need to be.

Has God been quiet lately? He may be waiting until
your sole desire is his presence in your life. Your best
course is to keep seeking and loving him. Because when
he does finally answer, it is going to be a very important
message, and you will not want to miss it.

*God, please do not let me miss your instruction. Rather,
help me to keep seeking you even when you are silent—
because you mean everything to me. Amen.*

The LORD is my strength and my shield; in him my heart trusts, and I am helped; my heart exults, and with my song I give thanks to him.

PSALM 28:7 ESV

THE BASIS FOR YOUR TRUST

*Ascribe to the Lord glory and strength. Give to
the Lord the glory due to His name; worship
the Lord in the beauty of holiness.*
PSALM 29:1–2 AMP

You have been encouraged to trust God; but why should
you be confident in his care? How can you depend upon

someone you have never seen?

Understand that your faith in
God is not to be blind or unsub-
stantiated. Rather, it should be
based on his faultless character.
He is all-powerful, completely
able to do whatever is necessary
to help you. He is all-knowing; his wisdom concerning
your situation and how to deliver you is flawless.

Friend, what challenge weighs on your heart today? Trust
God to help you. You have great reason for confidence
because of his wonderful character. So do as he says,
because he is willing and able to bring you the victory.

*God, you are so worthy of praise and adoration. I thank
you for your faultless character and great help to me.
I am truly blessed by your love. Amen.*

Above the floodwaters is God's throne from which his power flows, from which he rules the world. God makes his people strong. God gives his people peace.

PSALM 29:10–11 MSG

THE DARK BEFORE DAYLIGHT

*At night we may cry, but when morning
comes we will celebrate.*

PSALM 30:5 CEV

The hour is late, and you are exhausted. Anxiety is keeping you awake even though you realize you cannot fix things, at least not right now. The tears flow. How can  you live another day with this problem hanging over you? The situation seems as dark and hopeless as the night sky.

Friend, you simply cannot continue without rest. Your weariness is making your actions less effective and your situation appear more dismal. You need to sleep, to recuperate your mental, emotional, and physical strength. Understandably, it will take faith for you to shut your eyes; however, God will continue providing for you even while you slumber.

Therefore, rest in him. Expect him to work on your behalf. Because no matter how dire the situation, he can restore your joy by morning. Trust him.

*God, please calm my fears and give me rest. I want to
trust you, Lord. Please release me from these worries so I
can praise your matchless name. Amen.*

You have changed my sadness into a joyful dance. . . .
So I will not be silent; I will sing praise to you.
*L*ORD, *you are my God; I will give you thanks forever.*

PSALM **30:11–12** GNT

TOUGH WORLD, TENDER GOD

*You have seen my troubles, and you care about the
anguish of my soul. You have not handed me over to
my enemies but have set me in a safe place.*

PSALM 31:7–8 NLT

Trouble comes in many forms and finds everyone eventually. Some people feel like outcasts and never really learn

to fit in. Others face financial, physical, or relational problems that keep them in constant chaos. The world offers no solutions or mercy. On the contrary, people must constantly beware of those who would take advantage of their weaknesses.

Unfortunately, instead of turning to God, people question why he allows so

much suffering. Yet the reason there is such turmoil is that
sin is a painful reality in the world.

Friend, God longs to show you his loving care, but you
must stop clinging to the world and blaming him for your
hardships. Rather, embrace him. He will reveal the truth
and free you from your hurt.

*God, forgive me for blaming you for my troubles and
turning to the world for comfort. Help me to always
remember that only you can truly heal my heart. Amen.*

*Be strong, all who wait with hope for the L*ORD,
and let your heart be courageous.

PSALM 31:24 GOD'S **W**ORD

GOOD-BYE TO GUILT

I confessed my sins and told them all to you.
I said, "I'll tell the Lord each one of my sins."
Then you forgave me and took away my guilt.

PSALM 32:5 CEV

There are those who believe that humanity is inherently flawed, and in a sense, they are right. Sin corrupts from within, and people are powerless to break its influence over them.

Thankfully, you are not without hope. Though you cannot help yourself, you know the One who erases your guilt and releases you from its bondage. The problem you have is letting go. You somehow convince yourself that the wickedness within you is more than God can handle. However, that simply is not true.

Stop trying to earn what he has offered you freely. Embrace the good he wants to do in and through you.

God, thank you for forgiving me of my sins. You have
released me from my guilt and given me a clean heart.
I praise your holy and powerful name! Amen.

You are my hiding place; You shall preserve me from trouble; You shall surround me with songs of deliverance.

PSALM 32:7 NKJV

AN OUTPOURING OF BEAUTY

Sing for joy in the LORD, O you righteous ones;
praise is becoming to the upright.

PSALM 33:1 NASB

Would you consider yourself beautiful? For many, this is a painful question; however, it should not be. You see, every

culture has its standards for attractiveness, yet there are character attributes that are seen as universally lovely in every society. A woman who is loving, joyful, peaceful, patient, kind, good, faithful, gentle, and self-controlled is regarded as exquisite all over the world.

That is because these are traits created in you by God's Holy Spirit. They flow from you effortlessly when you live your life in obedience and adoration to him.

Would you like to be considered truly lovely? Then remember that you are most attractive when you are praising him and letting his beauty shine through you.

God, thank you for making me radiant with your beauty!
May adoration and praise flow from my life so all will
worship you and give you the glory. Amen.

Sing to Him a new song; play skillfully [on the strings] with a loud and joyful sound. For the word of the Lord is right; and all His work is done in faithfulness.

PSALM 33:3–4 AMP

FEAR NOT

*I sought the LORD, and he answered me
and delivered me from all my fears.*

PSALM 34:4 ESV

What are you afraid of? What anxieties keep you awake
at night, wondering what terrible news tomorrow will
bring? Fear is a very destructive emotion; it can make

everything in your life fall
apart.

That is why God not only
frees you from your difficulties, but from the power of fear
as well. How does he do so?
First John 4:18 explains,
"God's perfect love drives out
fear" (NCV). He teaches you that anything that enters
your life must first pass through his loving hand. If he
allows a difficult situation to affect you, then he will most
certainly use it for your good.

Therefore, do not be afraid. When you lie awake troubled by anxieties, turn your thoughts to his perfect love
and allow him to calm your heart.

*God, thank you for protecting me and teaching me
courage through your wonderful love. Truly, with you,
I have absolutely no reason to fear. Amen.*

Those who look to him for help will be radiant with joy; no shadow of shame will darken their faces.

PSALM 34:5 NLT

THE DRAMA QUEEN WITHIN

Do you want to live and enjoy a long life? Then don't say cruel things and don't tell lies. Do good instead of evil and try to live at peace.

PSALM 34:12–14 CEV

"Go ahead, get it out of your system," your friends urge during some trial. So you do. You allow the emotions to  pour forth. You spout things you do not really mean, and you blow your troubles out of proportion.

You feel better for a moment. Then the feelings come back stronger than ever, and they are even more painful and harder to shake off. What happened?

The problem is not that you have expressed your emotions; it is that you have allowed them to run amok. Now you are trapped by the drama you have created.

Express yourself to God and allow his wisdom to guide you. The path will lead you to peace.

God, I do not need drama in my life—I need your peace. Please forgive me for spouting off. Help me to deal with my emotions in a way that honors you. Amen.

The LORD is close to the brokenhearted, and he saves those whose spirits have been crushed. People who do what is right may have many problems, but the Lord will solve them all.

PSALM 34:18–19 NCV

EXCHANGING TRIALS FOR GLORY

My whole being will exclaim,
"Who is like you, O LORD?"
PSALM 35:10 NIV

If you are strong or gifted enough to accomplish a task, what room is there for God to work? If you can person-

ally guarantee a successful conclu-sion to the assignment you face, what need is there for faith?

That is why God will challenge you beyond what you can handle. It is only when you cannot manage your circumstances that you acknowledge God's hand. Any success you achieve is from God. Of course, no one likes

to relinquish control, but that is what it takes to see his astounding work in your life.

Are you committed to following him no matter what it takes? Are you willing to encounter trials in exchange for experiencing his glory? When you are, you will truly get to know him, and that is definitely worth it.

God, I want to know you, but I am afraid of losing control. Teach me to respond to situations in a way that honors you and helps me grow in your love. Amen.

Those who want the best for me, let them have the last word—a glad shout!—and say, over and over and over, "GOD is great—everything works together for good for his servant."

PSALM 35:27 MSG

REAL, ABUNDANT LIFE

With you is the fountain of life;
in your light do we see light.

Psalm 36:9 ESV

What does the perfect life look like to you? Perhaps you picture a life of wealth and luxury. Or maybe you desire

to be surrounded by loved ones, people who care deeply about you. Although there is nothing wrong with these dreams, when you finally reach them, you will most likely find that there is still something missing.

John 17:3 explains, "Eternal life is to know you, the only true God, and to know Jesus Christ" (CEV). That is because when you seek God, you will find a truly worthwhile life, not only full of purpose but also full of love, hope, and meaning.

Pursue God. Love him. Devote yourself to him. He will satisfy your heart's deepest desires.

God, I need you in my life. Your presence makes all things more wonderfully satisfying—including family, friendships, and all this life has to offer. Amen.

Your love, O LORD, reaches to the heavens, your faithfulness to the skies. . . . How priceless is your unfailing love! Both high and low among men find refuge in the shadow of your wings.

PSALM 36:5, 7 NIV

PATICENCE, FRIEND

Entrust your ways to the LORD. Trust him, and he
will act on your behalf. . . . Surrender yourself
to the LORD, and wait patiently for him.
PSALM 37:5, 7 GOD'S WORD

It can be very frustrating. You get ready to work, but the
inspiration is just not there. You need to get things done

to stay on track, but something prevents you from moving forward.

Friend, God is waiting for you to get
quiet before him, to cast aside your
worries and seek the peace of his
presence. After all, what you are
doing is for him; he is not going to

fail you. However, learning to trust him is more important
than whatever you must get done.

Therefore, take a deep breath and calm your heart.
Express your absolute confidence that he will do as he has
promised. He will help you in your work and provide the
desires of your heart. Wait patiently for him to inspire you.
He will certainly do wonderful things on your behalf.

Lord, waiting is a challenge! Help me to be patient. Help
me to know you better and trust you more so that I may
serve you wholeheartedly and please you. Amen.

Trust in the LORD, and do good; dwell in the land, and feed on His faithfulness. Delight yourself also in the LORD, and He shall give you the desires of your heart.

PSALM 37:3–4 NKJV

WORDS OF THE WISE

The godly offer good counsel;
they teach right from wrong.
PSALM 37:30 NLT

When you are hurting, a friend's timely counsel can be a precious gift. Yet how can you discern if what she is telling

you is godly and wise—or if it is foolish and destructive?

First, her words must line up with God's Word, never contradicting the principles of Scripture. Second, her instruction should direct you to the Lord and encourage you to honor him completely. Third, whether she is offering you comfort or correction, she should not be fishing for a certain response. Rather, she must be honest, compassionate, and tactful so you can grow in your faith.

Sometimes it will be obvious that a friend's advice is straight from God, but when it is not, turn her words over to him in prayer. He will certainly show you whether it is worthwhile counsel or not.

God, please help me discern whether the advice I receive
and give is godly and wise. I want to honor you, Lord,
especially in the counsel I give to others. Amen.

*Look at those who are honest and good, for a
wonderful future awaits those who love peace.*

PSALM 37:37 NLT

Merciful

God, be merciful to me because you are loving. Because you are always ready to be merciful, wipe out all my wrongs. Wash away all my guilt and make me clean again.

PSALM 51:1–2 NCV

DO THE GODLY HAVE BAD DAYS?

O Lord . . . my groaning has not been hidden from you. . . . I confess my guilt. My sin troubles me.
PSALM 38:9, 18 GOD'S WORD

With so many promises and blessings that come with knowing God, one may get the false impression that

there are no longer any trials or temptations for those who believe in him. However, that is not true.

God comprehends that you are not perfect. You are still going to make mistakes—dishonoring him and hurting yourself in the process. You still have things to learn.

Friend, do not allow the guilt of a bad day to defeat you. Rather, repent of your mistake and accept it for what it is—an opportunity for God's grace and instruction. Then embrace what he teaches so that the next time temptation comes knocking, you can do what is right.

God, thank you for your patience with me, for picking me up when I fall, and for putting me back on the path to righteousness. Truly you are good. Amen.

What I do, GOD, is wait for you,
wait for my Lord, my God—you will answer!

PSALM 38:15 MSG

A DIFFERENT FOCUS

*Lord, make me to know my end and [to appreciate] the
measure of my days—what it is; let me know and realize
how frail I am [how transient is my stay here].*
PSALM 39:4 AMP

Too often people base their happiness on a future experience—a career, a wedding, the birth of a child, or what

have you. They are utterly
convinced that they will
not be content or complete
without it. Unfortunately,
they are so focused on
tomorrow that they fail to
make the most of today,
and they miss the blessings God has for them.

Friend, is this you? Are you waiting for life to begin
when you get that great job, meet the perfect man, or
achieve some other goal? Then your focus is misplaced.

God has important things for you to do and people for
you to love today. So do not waste your life on fantasies.
Rather, devote it to the One who will make you truly
joyful and whole. The rest will come in its time.

*God, only you can truly make my life meaningful.
Please help me to focus on honoring you today
rather than the blessings of tomorrow. Amen.*

Lord, what do I wait for? My hope is in You.

PSALM 39:7 HCSB

LIFE AS HIS VESSEL

He put a new song in my mouth, a song of praise to our God. Many people will see this and worship him. Then they will trust the Lord.

PSALM 40:3 NCV

It is generally easier to believe the negative things people say about you rather than the positive. *Ugly. Stupid.*

Disgraceful. Worthless. These words make lasting wounds on your heart, and it is difficult to overcome them.

Yet remember, it is not what the vessel is made of that gives it value but what it contains. When you believe in God, he fills you, and your life becomes a vessel of praise to him. You have been completely changed. You no longer have any reason to feel shame, because God has provided you with a new identity based on his beauty, wisdom, holiness, and worth.

Friend, you have been emptied of your indignities and filled with God's glory. Let him shine through you so others can trust him as well.

God, you have changed me from inside out, and I praise your name! Thank you for giving me such hope, worth, beauty, wisdom, and holiness. Amen.

*Let all who seek you rejoice and be glad because
of you. Let those who love your salvation
continually say, "The LORD is great!"*

PSALM 40:16 GOD'S WORD

AN AMAZING FUTURE

You, LORD God, have done many wonderful things, and you have planned marvelous things for us. No one is like you! I would never be able to tell all you have done.

PSALM 40:5 CEV

This verse contains a wonderful promise: God has planned marvelous things for you. In fact, his vision for

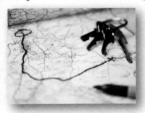

your future is infinitely higher and abundantly better than anything you could imagine.

If you are somewhat confused about what he is doing in your life—it is no wonder. You are not

supposed to figure it out or understand how all of your experiences fit together. Not yet, anyway. God is doing something through you that is so amazing it can only be achieved by his magnificent power and imagination.

Allow this hope to strengthen you today: Because of God's extraordinary love, the best is still ahead. His plans for your future are unfolding, and they are truly fantastic. So have faith, friend, honor him always, and praise his glorious name.

God, I can imagine some amazing things—but your plans are resplendently filled with your love, power, and brilliance. Praise your wonderful name! Amen.

I delight to do Your will, O my God;
Your Law is within my heart.

PSALM 40:8 NASB

REFLECTING HIS CHARACTER

Happy are those who are concerned for the poor;
the LORD will help them when they are in trouble.
PSALM 41:1 GNT

God has provided everything you have. When you
needed salvation, he gave it to you freely. When you were

desperate for his help and comfort, he
sent it to you without reservation.

He does this not only for your sake, but
for those around you as well. You see, it
is his desire that as you receive his compassion and encouragement, they will
transform you and you will grow in his
character. You become kindhearted and
giving as a result of your love and gratitude to the Lord.

Friend, do you give freely, reflecting God's character and
provision to others? God is generous and loving, and he
wants his people to be so as well. So today be his repre-
sentative and care for those in need just as he would.

God, thank you for your mercy and generosity. Help me to
meet others' needs with your sincere compassion so that
they can know you and praise your name. Amen.

By this I know that You favor and delight in me. . . .
You have upheld me in my integrity and
set me in Your presence forever.

PSALM 41:11–12 AMP

YOUR SOUL'S TRUE YEARNING

My soul thirsts for God, for the living God.
When shall I come and appear before God?
PSALM 42:2 NKJV

You cannot seem to fill that uneasy longing within. You go shopping, but it doesn't help. You eat something delicious, but that does not satisfy you either. You try socializing more to fill the emptiness, but soon you find that doesn't do it either.

It isn't your body, heart, or stomach that is crying out, it is your soul. It is the part of you that requires spiritual growth and refreshment. Friend, you need God. You need God more than you need food, clothing, sunshine, or shelter. Your Creator satisfies your yearning for purpose, worth, and eternity, teaching you his insight and inspiring you with his presence.

Neither the spoon nor the credit card can help you, but prayer and reading his Word can. So do not ignore this crucial need. Your thirst is for God. Drink and be filled.

God, thank you for satisfying the deep needs of my soul—
for inspiring me with your purpose and refreshing me
with you presence. You truly fill me with joy. Amen.

The LORD will send His faithful love by day;
His song will be with me in the night—
a prayer to the God of my life.

PSALM 42:8 HCSB

GOOD TIMES PAST

*My heart is breaking as I remember how it used
to be: I walked among the crowds of worshipers,
leading a great procession to the house of God.*

PSALM 42:4 NLT

Can you think of a time when your relationship with God
felt deeper and more meaningful? Maybe you remember

when your faith was new and his
presence seemed to permeate your
every activity. Alternatively, perhaps you recall an encounter with
him that powerfully transformed
your life.

Yet understand, it is dangerous to
enshrine experiences with God, believing your best times
with him are past. Your relationship with God is not just
about what happened yesterday, but it is about how you love
and obey him today.

Keep your eyes fixed on God always, and you will experience a more intimate relationship than you ever thought
possible.

*God, I want our relationship to be healthy and flourish.
Help me to seek you daily so our intimacy can grow
deeper all the days of my life. Amen.*

Why are you down in the dumps, dear soul?
Why are you crying the blues? Fix my
eyes on God—soon I'll be praising again.
He puts a smile on my face. He's my God.

PSALM 42:5 MSG

LEARNING TO LOVE HIM

I will go to the altar of God, to God my exceeding joy;
and upon the lyre I shall praise You, O God, my God.
PSALM 43:4 NASB

The student who studies to play an instrument with a mediocre teacher will take on the shortcomings of her

mentor. It is only through the patient training of a skilled maestro that she is able to unlearn any faulty technique and discover the true art of her instrument.

The same is true for love. Sometimes people are negatively influenced by those who first love them, and their devotion to God falls short. The wonderful thing about God is that he gladly teaches people how to love him.

Did you have a flawed example of love when you were growing up? Do not despair. The great Maestro will show you the most excellent way to express love and be loved in return. So learn from him, friend, and sing his praises with joy.

God, you are the great Maestro of my heart. Teach me to
love as you do, unconditionally, sacrificially, with joy
and trust. To you be all the glory. Amen.

Send your light and your truth. Let them guide me.
Let them bring me to your holy mountain and to
your dwelling place.

PSALM 43:3 GOD'S WORD

ALL YOU REALLY NEED

Not in my bow do I trust, nor can my sword save me. But you have saved us. . . . In God we have boasted continually, and we will give thanks to your name forever.

PSALM 44:6–8 ESV

King Jehoshaphat of Judah realized that his nation did not stand a chance against the invading armies of Ammon,

Moab, and Mount Seir. So he prayed, asking the Lord for instruction.

God's direction to him went against all conventional wisdom. Instead of fighting the enemy with swords and bows, the people of Judah were to worship the Lord with singing. So they did. They praised him as their enemies advanced. And miraculously, he won their battle for them.

Are you facing a challenge that seems overwhelming to you today? Seek God's guidance. His instructions may not make sense, but obey him anyway, doing exactly as he says. He will surely triumph in this battle for you.

God, I have been fretting because I do not have the resources for the challenge I face today. Thank you for showing me that all I need is to obey you. Amen.

It wasn't their power that gave them victory. But it was your great power and strength. You were with them because you loved them.

PSALM 44:3 NCV

HE CALLS YOU BEAUTIFUL

The king is enthralled by your beauty;
honor him, for he is your lord.

PSALM 45:11 NIV

Today before you look in the mirror and pick yourself apart, think about this wonderful truth: God finds you  lovely. He created every detail that makes you unique—your personality, giftedness, and traits—with loving care, and he is enthralled with what he has accomplished.

You are precious to God. Filled with potential, every facet of who you are is beautiful to him. Yet what he loves most about you is that your heart, which has been cleansed with his forgiveness and covered with his righteousness, now longs to know, honor, and obey him.

So as you look in the mirror, praise him for how he made you, even those things you wish you could change. Then gaze into his face and realize that your beauty is really a reflection of his.

God, how wonderful it is to be loved so deeply and completely. Fill my eyes with your magnificent face, and my heart with your wonderful love. Amen.

You love righteousness and hate wickedness;
therefore God, your God, has set you above your
companions by anointing you with the oil of joy.

PSALM 45:7 NIV

ASSURED IN HIS PRESENCE

God is within her, she will not fall;
God will help her at break of day.
PSALM 46:5 NIV

Assyrian soldiers were known for their ruthless obliteration of any nation that dared resist their progress. When

the invading army drew near to Jerusalem, King Hezekiah had a tough choice to make. Should he surrender unconditionally to the Assyrians in the hope of saving his people? Or should he trust God to deliver them?

In a leap of faith, Hezekiah chose the Lord. Psalm 46 is thought by some to be the song of triumph written when God honored Hezekiah's faithfulness and delivered Jerusalem.

Has God been leading you to make a very difficult decision? Like Jerusalem, you will not fall as long as you trust in God and obey him. So take the leap of faith and be confident that he will lead you victoriously.

O God, you know the struggle I am having with this
decision. Yet I will have faith and do as you say. Please
protect me, and lead me to victory. Amen.

*God is our Refuge and Strength [mighty and
impenetrable to temptation], a very present
and well-proved help in trouble.*

PSALM 46:1 AMP

STRENGTH FROM STILLNESS

*Cease striving and know that I am God; I will be
exalted among the nations, I will be exalted in the earth.*
PSALM 46:10 NASB

The swift pace and challenges of life can leave you weary
and disheartened if you never take time to rest in your

relationship with God. That is
why it is crucial for you to be
quiet before him, surrendering
yourself and your struggles to
him as an offering.

Be silent and relax, confident
that he can handle everything
that concerns you. Meditate on
his sufficiency. Surely nothing is
impossible for Almighty God—the glorious Creator of
heaven and earth. Receive his mighty strength and wonderful wisdom for every burden you carry.

It is in the stillness that God will give you the confidence
and endurance for everything that comes your way. So
know him, friend, and find peace.

*God, I sit before you in quiet expectation. Please help me
to be calm and focus on you. Fill me with your peace and
strength and I will praise your name. Amen.*

Come, behold the works of the LORD.

PSALM 46:8 NKJV

HIS RIGHTFUL PLACE

God is the king of the whole earth.
Make your best music for him!
PSALM 47:7 GOD'S WORD

When visiting heads of state, it is customary to bring a gift. Certainly no mediocre offering will do. You must present the dignitary with a meaningful item that repre-

sents your respect for them.

Unfortunately, most people do not approach God with the same reverence. Whereas people will offer their best to earthly leaders, they believe their Creator will be satisfied

with the leftovers. They give him a few seconds of prayer, a minute or two of Bible reading, and an honorable mention now and again, and they think it is enough.

When all other rulers have turned to dust, he remains Lord of all. God deserves your absolute best. So stop presenting him with halfhearted offerings. Give God his rightful place in your life and truly honor him.

God, please forgive my not honoring you as I should.
Help me to give you my very best today and every day—
just as you deserve. Amen.

Clap your hands, all you peoples! Shout to God with the voice of triumph! For the LORD Most High is awesome; He is a great King over all the earth.

PSALM 47:1–2 NKJV

ETERNITY IN YOUR HEART

As we have heard, so have we seen in the city of the
LORD of hosts, in the city of our God;
God will establish it forever.

PSALM 48:8 NKJV

Does it ever feel as if you simply do not belong in this world? As if you are longing for something beyond what exists here? You are not imagining things, and you are certainly not alone.

Hebrews 11:13, 16 explains that faithful people throughout the ages have "agreed that they were only strangers and foreigners on this earth . . . they were looking forward to a better home in heaven" (CEV).

You see, when you believe in God, he awakens the desire for eternity in you. Each time you sense that you are out of place here, it is because he's further along in the process of transforming you to live in heaven forever.

Whenever you feel like your heart is somewhere else—that is okay. Just remember, friend, you are not home yet.

God, thank you for preparing me for heaven. I may not
understand it all, but I praise you for establishing a
wonderful home for me with you forever. Amen.

This God, our God forever and ever—
He will lead us eternally.

PSALM 48:14 HCSB

Refuge

From the end of the earth I call to you when my heart is faint. Lead me to the rock that is higher than I, for you have been my refuge.

PSALM 61:2–3 ESV

WORTHY VENTURES

My mouth shall speak wisdom; the meditation
of my heart shall be understanding.
I will incline my ear to a proverb.

PSALM 49:3–4 ESV

As a beloved child of God, there are some activities that are not worthy of your time. Pursuing possessions that

quickly perish, holding grudges, fretting over the future, and achieving ambitions by unjust means, are all deeds that are unbecoming to one who belongs to the Lord.

Strengthening your relationship with God through prayer and Bible study, representing him faithfully in the

world, being a good example, and telling others about him so they can be freed from sin are all exercises that have enduring results in eternity.

You are a woman of worth, so do not waste your precious life on unworthy pursuits. Rather, do only things that honor God. Then you can be sure that every minute is time well spent.

God, I want to honor you. Please show me the activities
that merit my time and the ones that do not so
I can glorify you with my entire life. Amen.

*See what happens to those who trust in themselves,
the fate of those who are satisfied with their
wealth—they are doomed. . . . But God will rescue
me; he will save me from the power of death.*

PSALM 49:13–15 GNT

THE BALM OF THANKSGIVING

"Bring your thanks to God as a sacrifice, and keep your vows to the Most High. Call on me in times of trouble. I will rescue you, and you will honor me."
PSALM 50:14–15 GOD'S WORD

The Bible encourages you to give thanks to God in every situation, even in the circumstances that are difficult.

This shows your willingness to have faith in him even in the most trying areas of your life.

Yet you find that there are experiences and troubles that you just cannot trust him with. The wounds are too deep and the sacrifice too painful.

Friend, God understands. Yet he does not ask for gratitude for his sake. He does it to make you whole. He knows that when you praise him, it exposes the hidden injuries of your heart to his healing touch.

Therefore, friend, thank him, even when it is a sacrifice. His loving restoration is something you can truly be grateful for.

My God, you know how difficult this is for me. This area is so painful. Yet I will trust your loving touch. Thank you for healing me, my precious Lord. Amen.

He who sacrifices thank offerings honors me,
and he prepares the way so that I may
show him the salvation of God.

PSALM 50:23 NIV

READY TO RENEW

Wipe out all that I have done wrong. Create a clean heart in me, O God, and renew a faithful spirit within me.

PSALM 51:9–10 GOD'S WORD

Psalm 51 records David's repentance for committing adultery with Bathsheba and murdering her husband. It is

the profoundly moving prayer of a man devastated by the depth of his sin. Yet in the midst of his despair, he clung to the love and grace of God and refused to let go.

Perhaps you have been shocked at the temptations that have seized your own heart. You may have even fallen in sin, and your spirit is as broken as David's was. Remember, friend, just as God forgave and restored David, he will forgive and restore you if you will confess your sin and repent.

Do not lose hope. Rather, cling to God. Trust him, and he will not only cleanse your heart, but he will renew your spirit as well.

God, thank you for forgiving my sin and renewing my relationship with you. I cling to your love and rejoice in your wonderful mercy. Amen.

Restore the joy of your salvation to me, and provide me with a spirit of willing obedience. . . . O God, you do not despise a broken and sorrowful heart.

PSALM 51:12, 17 GOD'S WORD

BRIGHT FUTURE

Wash away all my guilt and make me clean again.
. . . Then I will teach your ways to those who do
wrong, and sinners will turn back to you.

PSALM 51:2, 13 NCV

If you have ever asked God to forgive your sin, then you
know how much relief it brings. Released from your
transgressions, you were no
longer oppressed by the stress
and guilt they caused you.
Rather, you were transformed
into a new creation with a clean,
peaceful heart and you regained
your hopefulness for a bright
future. Undoubtedly, such a wonderful liberation made
you feel like celebrating.

Hopefully you are not enjoying your liberty alone.

Today, tell others about God's forgiveness and salvation
so they can be liberated from their sin and experience his
peace. It is too wonderful a message to keep to yourself,
so share it with everyone you know.

God, I praise you for your astounding forgiveness. Help
me to tell others about your salvation so that they can
enjoy the same freedom that you have given to me. Amen.

*Save me from bloodguilt, O God, the God who saves
me, and my tongue will sing of your righteousness.*

PSALM 51:14 NIV

WHEN THINGS SEEM UNFAIR

I will thank You and confide in You forever, because You have done it [delivered me and kept me safe]. I will wait on, hope in and expect in Your name, for it is good.

PSALM 52:9 AMP

Before David ever took the throne of Israel, he had many heartbreaking experiences. At one point, he ran from

King Saul and asked for help from the priests of Nob. Although the priests did not know Saul was pursuing David, the king put them to death for aiding his enemy.

You can imagine how David felt when he heard what had transpired—in fact, Psalm 52 records his thoughts. It was so unfair—the priests were merely trying to help him. Why would God allow it?

Even when life does not seem fair, God is in control.

Are you experiencing circumstances that make no sense? Do not despair. Hope in God.

God, thank you for helping me. When things seem unfair, I will trust you—remaining confident that you will transform this situation for my good and your glory. Amen.

I am like a flourishing olive tree in the house of God; I trust in God's faithful love forever and ever.

PSALM 52:8 HCSB

WORTH REPEATING

*God looked down from heaven on all people to see if any-
one was wise, if anyone was looking to God for help.*

Whenever you read something more than once in
Scripture, it is because it is important. This is the case
with Psalm 53, which is strikingly similar to Psalm 14.

Its message is certainly worthy of
repetition—God peers down from
his throne in heaven, watching for
people who are looking for him.
He wants to answer the searching
heart and show his love to any who
call upon him.

Are you seeking God? Do you long to experience his
presence in a deep, meaningful way? Then realize that
this desire within you is one he answers with a resound-
ing "Yes!" He is gazing at you, friend, and he is delighted
that you want to know him. Surely he will reveal himself
to you in a powerful way.

*God, I want to love you with all my heart, soul, mind,
and strength. Thank you for making yourself known to
me and for teaching me your wonderful ways. Amen.*

*How happy the people of Israel will be when
God makes them prosperous again!*

PSALM 53:6 GNT

HIS CHERISHED NAME

I will give thanks to your name, O LORD, for it is good. For he has delivered me from every trouble.

PSALM 54:6–7 ESV

William Shakespeare wrote, "What's in a name? that which we call a rose by any other name would smell as

sweet." Yet when considering God's name, it carries with it meaning that should give you comfort and confidence.

Take heart that when you read the Bible and see "LORD" in all capitals; it is an indication that it is a transliteration of *Yahweh*, which means, "I AM." In God's name is his character—the declaration that he is the ever-present Lord, who will never fail you.

He is faithful, wise, all-powerful, loving, and able to help you no matter what happens—just as he has been throughout history and will always be forevermore. The One you love is worthy of adoration.

My God, the great I AM, thank you for being faithful and trustworthy in my life and in the lives of all your people. May your name be cherished forever. Amen.

*God, save me by Your name, and
vindicate me by Your might!*

Psalm 54:1 HCSB

A FAITHFUL SOUNDING BOARD

*Give ear to my prayer, O God. . . . Give heed to
me and answer me; I am restless in my
complaint and am surely distracted.*

PSALM 55:1–2 NASB

The troubles come from every side, leaving you almost
paralyzed due to their intensity. You try to concentrate—

to get something done. However,
the problems you face bombard
your thoughts until you cannot
separate one from another.

You are weary, but cannot sleep.
You want to escape, but feel so
bound by the situation that you
cannot take your mind off it. You think no one could
possibly understand the toll it is taking on your soul.

However, there is One who does.

Friend, no matter what troubles you are facing, there is
no reason for despair. God hears you and will help you.
Call to him—lay your burdens at his feet. He is always
available to speak peace to your soul.

*God, thank you for understanding the terrible stress I am
experiencing and for listening to my prayers. And thank
you, dear Lord, for helping me as only you can. Amen.*

I call to God; God will help me. At dusk, dawn, and
noon I sigh deep sighs—he hears, he rescues.

PSALM 55:16–17 MSG

LET GO

Give your burdens to the L<small>ORD</small>, and he will take care of you. He will not permit the godly to slip and fall.

P<small>SALM</small> 55:22 NLT

There are some issues so personal that you feel you cannot give them up—not even to God. The thought of entrusting your beloved burden to his care is more than you can

handle. It is as if you would be allowing a piece of your heart to be torn from you.

Friend, let go. You have made this situation an idol, and you are clinging to it as if it could make you happy. Yet all that it has brought you is heartache.

Your battle is not with God, it is with yourself. Moreover, if you release this burden to him, he will take care of it better than you ever could. He will also heal you of all the pain it has caused you.

God, it is so difficult for me to relinquish control in this area. Nevertheless, I also know it will destroy me if I do not. Please help me—overcome my fears and teach me to trust. Amen.

He will redeem my soul in peace from the battle which is against me.

PSALM 55:18 NASB

IN THE PROPER PERSPECTIVE

By [the help of] God I will praise His word; on God I lean, rely, and confidently put my trust; I will not fear. What can man, who is flesh, do to me?

PSALM 56:4 AMP

Sometimes the negative words of others can be devastating. Because of them, you struggle with thoughts of

doubt, fear, or condemnation. However, the psalmist learned how to put the words of others in the proper perspective, and you can too.

When you believe in Jesus Christ as your Savior, you gain a fresh sense of unshakable hope and peace. The connection you have with him empowers you to stand firm against the most deceptive thought or attack. You discover how to say as the psalmist did, "I will not fear!" because you know that your Lord defends you.

Open your heart and mind to God's personal love and care for you. You will not be disappointed.

God, thank you for providing the hope I need to get through every situation. I will find hope and peace in your word. Amen.

You know how troubled I am; you have kept a record of my tears. . . . You have rescued me from death and kept me from defeat. And so I walk in the presence of God, in the light that shines on the living.

PSALM 56:8, 13 GNT

FOR HIS GLORY

Be exalted, O God, above the highest heavens!
May your glory shine over all the earth.
<small>PSALM 57:5 NLT</small>

There will be times when it is hard to contain the love you feel for God. Sunshine warms your face, a gentle breeze blows softly, and suddenly you are reminded of all  the times you have experienced his blessings. They are more than you can number.

He sustains you when trouble comes. He moves quickly to lift you up whenever you fall and cry out to him. He protects you as you drive along busy thoroughfares. When you wonder if he is listening to the prayers of your heart, he shows up in some miraculous way, letting you know that he hears every word.

He is God, and the earth is full of his glory. He also is the Lord who loves you with an everlasting love. So trust him, because he is truly faithful.

I bow down before you, Lord. I am in awe of your
greatness and in wonder of your infinite love.
Thank you for your ceaseless grace. Amen.

I cry out to God Most High, to God who fulfills his purpose for me.

PSALM 57:2 ESV

JUSTICE SERVED

*The godly will rejoice when
they see injustice avenged.*
PSALM 58:10 NLT

Does it ever seem as if the unrighteous get away with
their terrible schemes, while you are always caught no
matter what mistake you make?

The truth is, no one really gets away
with anything. Sin has many consequences, and God holds each person
accountable for his or her actions.
However, he does not want you
dwelling on how and when he will
move against the unjust. Rather, he
calls you to be mindful of his ability
to deal with every situation. He is in control, and in his
perfect timing every wrong will be addressed.

He also wants you to pray for those who are trapped in
sin—because it is only when they know him that they
will be able to escape from its terrible grasp.

*God, teach me to pray for those who do not know you
and to act wisely as I live my life for you. I praise
you for righting every wrong. Amen.*

Everyone will say, "It's true! Good people are rewarded. God does rule the earth with justice."

PSALM 58:11 CEV

THROUGH HIM YOU WON'T FAIL

O my Strength, I watch for you; you, O God, are my fortress, my loving God. God will go before me.
PSALM 59:9–10 NIV

You face many challenges every day—some are exciting, some routine, and others may be quite difficult. While  there are times of instability that will assail your life, there is one truth that never changes: God is your eternal strength and your present help. Nothing you face takes him by surprise.

God has never been unfaithful to you, and he never will be. If he has asked you to wait for his answer to come, then it is because he has something far better for you than you can imagine.

Thoughts of doubt may tempt you to believe that he is not watching over your life; however, if he knows when a sparrow falls to the earth, then he certainly knows your every need.

God, thank you for loving me and for walking with me each moment of every day. No matter what I face, I know that you will help me through the day. Amen.

*You've been a safe place for me. . . . Strong God,
I'm watching you do it, I can always count
on you—God, my dependable love.*

PSALM 59:16–17 MSG

YOUR NOT-SO-SECRET WEAPON

With God's help we will do mighty things.
PSALM 60:12 NLT

At first glance, a task may seem too great for you. You try to make a schedule, but confusion and fear set in. Before

you know it, you feel tempted to run. However, deep within your heart, God is saying, "Stay where you are. Trust me. I'll help you."

God's desire is to guide you at every turn in life, and he has promised to lead you past places of difficulty and extreme pressure in order to prove his faithfulness. You never have to be afraid, because he promises to provide all you need.

Are you facing an overwhelming challenge today? Have faith in the One who has all you need to achieve the victory. He will not fail you; rather, he will lead you to triumph—so trust him.

God, there are times when I feel overwhelmed by the circumstances of life, but I know you have promised to do mighty things in and through me when I trust you. Amen.

Use your powerful arm and give us victory.
Then the people you love will be safe.

PSALM 60:5 CEV

Strength

My flesh and my heart may fail, but God is the strength of my heart and my portion forever.

PSALM 73:26 ESV

A SOLID PLACE TO STAND

From the end of the earth I will cry to You,
when my heart is overwhelmed; lead me
to the rock that is higher than I.

PSALM 61:2 NKJV

At times you may lose your perspective about a situation because it is so overwhelming and earth-shattering.

Perhaps you have done something that cannot be fixed, and the realization of your mistake is taking you on a downward spiral of disappointment. God knows your heart, and he is willing to come to your aid.

On several occasions, David's confidence was shaken by his enemies, but the Lord repeatedly sustained him and gave him the victory.

Is your world being shaken by a tremendous challenge? Experiencing God's presence provided David with the stability and strength he needed to continue, and the same can be true for you.

God, please help me to sense your presence and rest in
your care. Thank you for giving me a solid place to stand
though the world around me quakes. Amen.

You have been a refuge for me, a strong tower in the face of the enemy. I will live in Your tent forever and take refuge under the shelter of Your wings.

PSALM 61:3–4 HCSB

A DAILY NEED

For God alone, O my soul, wait in silence, for my hope is from him. He only is my rock and my salvation, my fortress; I shall not be shaken.

PSALM 62:5–6 ESV

Every day, you will face challenges—some of them are simple to solve, while others are more trying. There will be

times when you will want to rush ahead of God, even though you do not have a clear plan.

However, he has allowed that difficulty so that you will learn to trust him at a deeper level—seeking him consistently for your needs. His timing in your situation is perfect, and if you move too quickly, you risk missing his best.

If you seek him daily and wait for him to work on your behalf, you will discover that your waiting is not in vain. Therefore, when trouble comes, ask him to show you how to deal with the matter and allow him to draw you even closer through it.

God, teach me to wait for your very best and to rest in the safety of your care. Every day I will seek your face and trust you to lead me. Amen.

Trust God, my friends, and always tell him each one of your concerns. God is our place of safety.

PSALM 62:8 CEV

UNTIL YOUR SOUL IS SATISFIED

O God, you are my God, and I long for you. My whole being desires you; like a dry, worn-out, and waterless land, my soul is thirsty for you.

PSALM 63:1 GNT

Responsibilities and struggles can drain your energy and emotions. Trials threaten to steal your hope and joy. You

survey the circumstances of your life and wonder how any good can come from what you are experiencing. But it can. When God is involved, there is always the potential for hope and blessing.

Problems are a natural part of life. Without much warning, stress can build, and before you know it, you are crying out for help. However, instead of cowering in fear, the psalmist used his trying situation as an opportunity to express his deep commitment to God.

Praise God for satisfying your soul, and express your trust that he will work things out for your good.

God, thank you for inviting me to experience your wonderful love. I long to know you better and experience your encouraging, satisfying presence. Amen.

You satisfy me more than the richest feast.
I will praise you with songs of joy.

PSALM 63:5 NLT

FOCUSED CONTEMPLATION

*I think about you before I go to sleep, and my
thoughts turn to you during the night.*

PSALM 63:6 CEV

One of the most effective things you can do to better
your life is to go to bed praising God for his goodness.

Doing this lays the groundwork for
gratitude, thanksgiving, and praise at
morning's first light.

Why is it important for you to
remember God's faithfulness?

Because recalling his goodness moti-
vates you to trust him for the future.
Remembering the times he has forgiven you teaches you to be honest
and admit your need for him. Realizing that he is at
work in your life gives you hope for the day to come.

It is easy to forget all the wonderful things God has
done. But when you focus on his goodness, it strength-
ens your spirit and helps you to turn to him quickly no
matter what may arise.

*Lord, help me focus on your unfailing love and praise you
with all my might. In your goodness and grace I will rest
peacefully, for you, Lord, are my hope. Amen.*

My whole being follows hard after You and clings closely to You; Your right hand upholds me.

PSALM 63:8 AMP

HIS HEALING ARROWS

Both the inward thought and the heart of man are deep. But God shall shoot at them with an arrow.

PSALM 64:6–7 NKJV

Have you ever gotten up in the morning and remembered some deed done to you as if it just happened? You

try to shake off the memory, but you walk around all day feeling as though you're under a cloud of anger.

God does not want your bitterness to rob you of the power and joy he has for you. That is why he will target it like a bowman with an arrow, so that you will deal with the issue consuming your thoughts, energy, and emotions.

It is easy to cling to feelings of unforgiveness, anger, or resentment, but God calls you to do the opposite—to forgive and move beyond the hurt. When you let go of past sorrows, you are free to accept the blessings he has for you.

Lord, I am in awe of your awesome love. Thank you for revealing my old wounds and healing me of their pain. Truly you are wonderful! Amen.

*Then all men will fear, and they will declare the
work of God, and will consider what He has done.*

PSALM 64:9 NASB

THE PRIVILEGE OF HIS PRESENCE

How happy is the one You choose and bring near to live in Your courts! We will be satisfied with the goodness of Your house, the holiness of Your temple.

PSALM 65:4 HCSB

God will challenge you to do many wonderful things in this life—he will encourage you to launch out in faith with

the tasks he calls you to do. But there is something that brings an even greater degree of satisfaction than anything you can experience on a human level, and that is time spent in quiet devotion to him.

Though your life may seem too full to take time to be alone with

him, consider this: He is never too busy to be with you. His one consuming desire is for you to know him. When you begin to do this, even the smallest of activities will take on new meaning.

So spend time with him today and enjoy the awesome privilege of being in his presence. Surely it will be the best time you have all day!

God, for far too long, I have dismissed your efforts to touch my heart. Please open my life up to you so I may experience all you have for me. Amen.

You answer us in amazing ways, God our Savior. People everywhere on the earth and beyond the sea trust you.

PSALM 65:5–6 NCV

IMPOSSIBILITIES

Take a good look at God's wonders—they'll take your breath away. He converted sea to dry land; travelers crossed the river on foot. Now isn't that cause for a song?
PSALM 66:5–6 MSG

The night the storm broke out on the Sea of Galilee, the wind picked up without warning. Then the waves began

to swell, and a hard rain beat down. Fear consumed the disciples' minds and hearts. How could they possibly survive the tempest?

Yet their anxiety was unfounded, because Jesus was with them. When their cries woke him, Jesus stood up and did the impossible—he commanded the wind and the waves to be still, and both obeyed.

The same is true for you whenever you experience the overwhelming storms of life. Though they arise unexpectedly, there is no reason to fear, because the Lord is with you.

Words cannot express my love for you, Lord. You are my refuge, and I am overwhelmed by your greatness and humbled by your love for me. Amen.

Bless our God, you peoples!
And make the voice of His
praise to be heard, who keeps
our soul among the living,
and does not allow our feet to
be moved. For You, O God,
have tested us; You have
refined us as silver is refined.

PSALM 66:8–10 NKJV

TO ALL PEOPLE

*God blesses us so people all over
the earth will fear him.*

PSALM 67:7 NCV

Whether you realize it or not, showing up at church on
Sunday is not the only way to express your love for God.

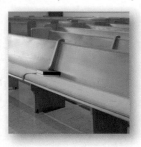

Your life is a living testimony to
others. Through your words and
actions, you reflect your core
beliefs, desires, faith, and fears.

When you care for another person freely rather than out of obligation, you are expressing God's
love. When you tell someone
about the reason for the hope you have, you honor God.

Do you view those around you as he views them—with
love, respect, and compassion? Do you share your blessings with them so that they will know the Savior? God
knows your heart and how you choose to live each day.
Therefore, honor him with everything you say and do so
that others may know him and be saved.

*My greatest desire, God, is for others to see you in and
through my life. Help me to share your love with
everyone I meet. Amen.*

Our God, be kind and bless us! Be pleased and smile. Then everyone on earth will learn to follow you, and all nations will see your power to save us.

PSALM 67:1–2 CEV

HIS TO LOVE

The God who is in his holy dwelling place is the
father of the fatherless and the defender of widows.
God places lonely people in families.

PSALM 68:5–6 GOD'S WORD

Have you truly opened your heart to the wondrous love
that God has for you? You may say, "Oh, I know he loves

me," but do you realize that his
love for you is so great that he
thinks about you constantly? He
longs to give you good things,
and when your heart is turned
toward him in devotion, he is
blessed.

You do not have to wait until you "feel" the love of
God—his love is a reality that is always present with you.
No sin can prevent him from loving you, and nothing is
greater or has more power than his love. Rather, he gives
his wonderful love to you freely, unconditionally; and the
closer you grow in your relationship with him, the more
you learn how faithful, strong, and true his care for you
really is.

Draw me ever nearer to you, Lord, so that I will know
the fullness of your love. In you I hope, and I
give myself to you wholeheartedly. Amen.

Thanks be to the Lord, who daily carries our burdens for us. God is our salvation.

PSALM 68:19 GOD'S WORD

WORTHY OF A WOMAN'S VOICE

*The Lord gave the command; a great company
of women brought the good news.*
PSALM 68:11 HCSB

Jesus was very aware of the spiritual devotion of the
women who followed him. He knew they were commit-

ted to God and wanted to serve
him in far greater ways than
the social climate of their society allowed. Mary of Bethany
sat at his feet listening as he
taught God's truth. Her greatest need was satisfied in
Christ's presence. She was a true believer—fully committed and determined to worship the Savior.

God uses women to tell others about his power to save
and heal the wounds that sin has wrought. Mary soaked
up every word spoken to her by the Savior, and you can
do the same. When opportunities come, you will be prepared to serve because you have been with the Lord.

*Shape my life, Lord God. Teach me your ways and your
Word. Use me in other people's lives for your glory.
And let my life be a psalm of praise to you. Amen.*

*Let the godly rejoice. Let them be glad in God's presence.
Let them be filled with joy. Sing praises to God and to
his name! Sing loud praises to him who rides the clouds.
His name is the Lord—rejoice in his presence!*

PSALM 68:3–4 NLT

GOD'S VICTORY OVER SELF-DEFEAT

My sins, O God, are not hidden from you; you know how foolish I have been. Don't let me bring shame on those who trust in you, Sovereign LORD Almighty!

PSALM 69:5–6 GNT

When you become aware of your potential to stray from God's love, you may feel shocked and even disappointed.

Temptations can entangle you, and sin can settle deep within your heart—preventing you from enjoying a close relationship with God.

It is easy to spot the signs of spiritual compromise in your life—you justify the sin and temptation, feel that you need to rush about rather than rest in God's presence, and give God and others a list of excuses about why your devotion is off course.

Nothing is more important than your relationship with him. In addition, when you lay aside your sin and go to him with a heart of devotion, you will notice a difference. Your life will be marked by peace and joy.

God, I know my tendency to self-destruct through sin and moral compromise. Please keep me from straying in my love toward you. Amen.

O God, in the greatness of
Your lovingkindness, answer
me with Your saving truth. . . .
The humble have seen it
and are glad; you who seek
God, let your heart revive.

PSALM 69:13, 32 NASB

I NEED YOU RIGHT NOW!

I am poor and needy; make haste to me, O God! You are
my help and my deliverer; O LORD, do not delay.

PSALM 70:5 NKJV

Have you ever noticed that sometimes when you try your
hardest to make something work, it turns out wrong?

These are often the times when God
allows you to face difficulty in order to
teach you to trust him more deeply.

By spending time with him in prayer —
listing your concerns, desires, and
needs — you are telling him that you
need him. Nothing touches his heart
more profoundly than hearing your sin-
cere prayer: "Father God, I can't do this on my own. I need
you." Such humility immediately stirs his compassion.

Friend, always remember that you can reach your goals by
keeping your heart set on him. So call to him. He is certainly ready to respond and will send the wisdom you need
for success.

God, I know there are times when I rush ahead of you.
I'm sorry. I confess my need and ask you to step into my
situation so I will have your infinite support. Amen.

*Let all who love your saving way say
over and over, "God is mighty!"*

PSALM 70:4 MSG

LOOKING UP TO YOU

*I am an example to many people, because
you are my strong protection.*

PSALM 71:7 NCV

Parents often laugh about the way their small children
pick up phrases they hear around the house—which are

often repeated at inopportune
times. Yet children are innocent
and just want to be like their
mom or dad.

You, on the other hand, are not a
child any longer, but still pick up
habits—good and bad—from
friends, co-workers, and others.

However, God has commanded that you set his Word as
your standard for living, obeying anything he commands
you to do.

Friend, just as the Lord expects you to set a godly pat-
tern for your loved ones, he also wants you to follow his
holy example. Therefore, look to him and imitate his
honorable character.

*God, forgive me for the times I have compromised my
testimony of your love. I know what is right, and I ask
that you help me to live in step with your truth. Amen.*

You will make me truly great
and take my sorrow away.

PSALM 71:21 CEV

WHOM DO YOU FOLLOW?

Give the gift of wise rule to the king,
O God. . . . May he judge your people rightly,
be honorable to your meek and lowly.

PSALM 72:1–2 MSG

Every day you receive many messages—people expressing their opinions on the television, radio, and in conversation.

Many have strong views and make viable cases for why you should have the same outlook as theirs. God cautions you to be wise and not believe all you hear.

God is straightforward in his approach to right and wrong—and you can be sure that anything that contradicts his Word is false and destructive. So do not get caught in the trap of thinking he does not really care what you do. He will not ignore your unfaithfulness.

The Lord has only the best in mind for your life, and he is motivated to see you enjoy it. However, it all begins with your obedience to him. Therefore, do as he says, because he really is worth following.

Lord God, you are truly a worthy leader, and I love your
ways. Please help me to embrace your truth and
to apply it correctly to my life. Amen.

*Praise be to the LORD God, the God of Israel,
who alone does marvelous deeds. Praise be to his
glorious name forever; may the whole
earth be filled with his glory.*

PSALM 72:18–19 NIV

Most High

May they know that You alone—whose name is Yahweh—are the Most High over all the earth.

PSALM 83:18 HCSB

IT ISN'T FAIR!

*I had nearly lost confidence; my faith was almost
gone because I was jealous of the proud when
I saw that things go well for the wicked.*

PSALM 73:2–3 GNT

There are times when life seems unjust, and you will have
to find a way to deal with what you have experienced.

People can do and say things that
are reckless and cruel. However,
whenever you feel ignored or
rejected, you have an important
choice to make: Either you can
become bitter or you can become
better. You can stew in your anger
or move on with the knowledge of
God's personal love for you.

God's priceless comfort can soften the impact of others'
thoughtless words and deeds. So keep your eyes on him.
Listen for his voice of encouragement and be willing to
forgive those who have hurt you. This is what Jesus did—
he forgave because he knew those who accused him did
not know the truth.

*God, thank you for understanding my hurts and my
feelings. Help me to do the same for others when
they act without reason or care. Amen.*

*In heaven I have only you, and on this earth you
are all I want. My body and mind may fail,
but you are my strength and my choice forever.*

PSALM 73:25–26 CEV

THE GREAT ARCHITECT

The day is Yours, also the night; You established the moon and the sun. You set all the boundaries of the earth.

PSALM 74:16–17 HCSB

With the changing political climate of our world, it would be easy to wonder if God is in control. The answer is yes.

The One who established the boundaries for the land and sea, and set the moon and stars in their places, watches over you.

When life appears to be spiraling out of control, you can be assured that God is not affected. Sudden changes do not surprise or move him—he remains the same yesterday, today, and forever.

When problems come, your first reaction may be one of anxiety. But God is sovereign, and he challenges you to recall the times he has kept you safe, protected your heart, and provided for every need you have. Always remember, nothing is too difficult for him to handle. No, friend— nothing at all.

God, I want a glimpse of your greatness. Whether changes occur in my life or on the world stage, I will watch for your sovereign hand and trust you always. Amen.

God my king is from ancient times,
performing saving acts on the earth.

PSALM 74:12 HCSB

THE SOURCE OF SUCCESS

Not from the east nor from the west nor from the south come promotion and lifting up. But God is the Judge! He puts down one and lifts up another.

PSALM 75:6–7 AMP

God waits for the perfect time to work. Up until the moment you see him in action, you may fear he's forgot-

ten the situations that weigh so heavily on your heart. He knows exactly what he is doing—and success is forthcoming.

In time, you will see how he has been working in the unseen. However, his instruction to you right now is a simple command to be steadfast and true to him. In other words, do not forfeit your faith. Even though you do not see the evidence of his hand at work, he is committed to honoring his promises to you.

God has a plan, and at the right moment, you will see it unfold. He will work all things together for your good in due time.

Lord, forgive me for the times that I forget that you are omniscient and aware of all that is taking place. I know you will accomplish your will. Amen.

God says, "I will break the strength of the wicked,
but I will increase the power of the godly."

PSALM 75:10 NLT

GOOD FEAR?

You alone must be feared!
Psalm 76:7 God's Word

The sense of fear the psalmist is writing about is a reverent fear that honors God. It has nothing to do with being so frightened that you turn and run away from him.

Adam and Eve hid because they had disobeyed God. They were afraid he was going to punish them, because sin always demands a payment for the wrong that has been done.

Jesus Christ paid the ultimate price for your sin at the cross. You do not have to hide from him or anxiously wait for him to punish you. When you seek him, he faithfully forgives and restores you.

God never wants you to dread his presence; rather, he wants the respect that grows from love. Therefore, fear him—in the good way. Because that is the fear that leads to salvation.

Jesus, thank you for forgiving my sin and for teaching me the holy reverence that leads to salvation. Help me to always rest in your care and holy presence. Amen.

All who live on this earth
were terrified and silent
when you took over as
judge, ready to rescue
everyone in need.

PSALM 76:8–9 CEV

WITH HISTORY AS A GUIDE

*You are the God who works wonders; you have
made known your might among the peoples.*
PSALM 77:14 ESV

The Bible is full of stories of faith—of people trapped in
terrible situations but who subsequently triumph because

of the Lord.

Perhaps like them, you are facing a problem that seems overwhelming. No one
understands the way you feel, and the
more you try to explain your circumstances, the more you are misunderstood.

Yet God knows exactly what you are fac-
ing, and he understands your fears. He knows when you
feel tempted to give up and has promised never to abandon you.

Just as he helped the saints throughout history, he can help
you as well. Therefore, trust him. He is just as powerful,
faithful, and wise today as when he delivered them, and
surely he will give you the victory as well.

*God, it is easy to trust you in times of sunshine, but help
me to have faith in the storm by reminding me of your
faithful works throughout the ages. Amen.*

I will remember your great deeds, Lord; I will recall the wonders you did in the past. I will think about all that you have done; I will meditate on all your mighty acts.

PSALM 77:11–12 GNT

PROACTIVE OR REACTIVE?

We will tell to the generation to come the praise-worthy deeds of the Lord, and His might, and the wonderful works that He has performed.

PSALM 78:4 AMP

Your life is a testimony of the way God works. People will learn whether they can truly trust the Lord by observing

how you handle moments of joy as well as times of sorrow.

Friend, when you battle hard-ships and obstacles, do you still demonstrate faith in your unshakable God? There were times when Moses, David, Paul, and the disciples experienced terrible pressure. Each one refused to give up or react negatively.

Rather, they were proactive—they not only honored the Lord and grew in their faith, but many others came to know him through their excellent example.

The same can be true for you, but you must decide to trust him in every situation.

Lord, I choose to trust you today and refuse to believe or respond to any and every thought of spiritual defeat.

He commanded our fathers, that they should make them known to their children . . . that they may set their hope in God, and not forget the works of God, but keep His commandments.

PSALM 78:5, 7 NKJV

UNEXPECTED ANSWERS

God made water flow from rocks he split open in the desert, and his people drank freely, as though from a lake. He made streams gush out like rivers from rocks.

PSALM 78:15–16 CEV

Here is one of the most exciting things about God: He does not always answer your prayers the same way. Just

when you think you understand how he will solve a problem, he takes a different route. This is why having faith is so important.

Always make sure that whatever you are doing is in line with the principles of his Word, but also allow him to be God—submit to him whenever he reshapes your plans even when you do not comprehend why he is leading you in a certain way. Never try to box him in with your expectations.

Because you will find that when you think you know all there is to know about him, he will do something far better than you could have ever imagined.

God, I love the way you surprise me with your goodness. Help me to always remain hopeful—anticipating your answers from unexpected places. Amen.

They remembered that God was their rock,
that the Most High was their defender.

PSALM 78:35 GOD'S WORD

HUMAN NATURE

Their hearts were not really loyal to God. . . . Still God was merciful. . . . He remembered that they were only human, like a wind that blows and does not come back.

PSALM 78:37–39 NCV

Even when you are unfaithful, God never stops loving you. He loves you with an enduring love that is both infi-

nite and unconditional. You cannot do anything to derail His love for you.

Sin harms your fellowship with him because it produces feelings of guilt and shame and causes you to wonder if he still cares for

you. Yet understand, although he will not approve of sin, he will never withhold His love from you.

So how do you handle the times when your human nature tempts you to yield to sin? The best course of action is to ask God to teach you more about his love. Because when you understand how great his love for you is, you will never want to drift in your devotion to him.

God, I want to honor you. Thank you for not holding my past against me. Thank you for forgiving me, loving me, and making me new. Amen.

[God] led His own people forth like sheep and guided them [with a shepherd's care] like a flock in the wilderness. And He led them on safely and in confident trust, so that they feared not.

PSALM 78:52–53 AMP

BREAKING DESTRUCTIVE CYCLES

Do not hold us guilty for the sins of our ancestors!
Let your compassion quickly meet our needs,
for we are on the brink of despair.

PSALM 79:8 NLT

You can change the way you respond to life's trials and temptations, but you cannot do it alone. You need God's encouraging truth to make the switch from failure to success.

Many people think this is impossible. They look at the shortcomings of their parents or other family members and are tempted to think, *I am just like them. I will never change.*

God did not want the nation of Israel to be defeated by the sins of their ancestors. He had a better plan in mind for them. Because of His great love and mercy, they could overcome every obstacle, and you can do the same when you surrender your life to him.

God, I want to be the very best I can be. Therefore, I
choose not to dwell on thoughts of defeat or failure.
Rather, I rejoice that your life flows through me. Amen.

Then we, your people, the ones you love and care for, will thank you over and over and over. We'll tell everyone we meet how wonderful you are, how praiseworthy you are!

PSALM 79:13 MSG

BY THE LIGHT OF HIS FACE

We shall not turn back from you; give us life, and we will call upon your name! Restore us, O LORD God of hosts! Let your face shine, that we may be saved!

PSALM 80:18–19 ESV

About Jesus, John 1:4–5 (NLT) reports, "His life brought light to everyone. The light shines in the darkness, and

the darkness can never extinguish it." The light of God's love and salvation can never be quenched.

When you are lonely, draw near to the Lord and he will brighten your day. When sorrow tries to settle in around you and tempt you to feel discouraged, lost, or forgotten, read His Word and ask him to illuminate your life. He will do it—he will speak to your heart and remind you that you are not alone.

When you encounter emotional clouds or rain, take a moment to ask God to light your way with his everlasting hope. He always answers the prayers of His children.

Lord, illuminate my life with your unquenchable love and hope. I praise you that all fear and darkness flees when your light shines on my heart. Amen.

*O Shepherd of Israel . . . You who dwell
between the cherubim, shine forth!*

PSALM 80:1 NKJV

HIS VERY BEST

"Oh that My people would listen to Me. . . .
I would feed you with the finest of the wheat, and
with honey from the rock I would satisfy you."
PSALM 81:13, 16 NASB

Many people spend a great deal of time and money trying to find a way to feel safe, secure, happy, and peaceful.

However, nothing you do apart from Jesus Christ has the ability to satisfy all of your needs and desires.

Large sums of money can vanish. People can walk away. Positions of power and fame can end in disgrace. Nothing this world has to offer can ensure future success or security. The one thing you can bank on is this: When God tells you he will satisfy you with the finest of wheat, he will give you his very best.

God withholds nothing from you. All that you need you will have, and you will never lack for anything.

At times it is hard to imagine how you will meet
all my needs, but, Lord, you always do—and your
provision is always perfect! Amen.

I took the world off your shoulders, freed you from a
life of hard labor. You called to me in your pain;
I got you out of a bad place. I answered
you from where the thunder hides.

PSALM 81:6–7 MSG

Light shines on those who do right; joy belongs to those who are honest. Rejoice in the LORD, you who do right. Praise his holy name.

PSALM 97:11–12 NCV

A PERSONAL RESPONSIBILITY

*Defend the weak and the orphans; defend
the rights of the poor and suffering.*
PSALM 82:3 NCV

The enemy of your soul cannot defeat you—not as long
as Jesus is guarding your life. Nothing is more powerful

than Christ's ability to sustain you.
He is all-knowing and all-powerful. No force on this earth can overwhelm you when you are walking
in fellowship with him.

However, when you choose to dis-
obey him and strike out on your
own, you will receive only what you
can produce. You also will expose yourself to the enemy's
sinister attacks.

Jesus promises to defend you and to fight on your behalf,
but only if you are surrendered to his manner of protecting you. Therefore, do not put yourself in harm's way.
Seek the Savior, who has promised to bless and keep
you, because he is faithful to give you the victory.

*Lord, keep me close to you. Make me aware of my
weaknesses so I can surrender them to you. Amen.*

Rescue weak and needy people. Help them escape the power of wicked people.

PSALM 82:4 GOD'S WORD

YOUR TRUSTWORTHY GOD

May they know that You alone—whose name is Yahweh—are the Most High over all the earth.

PSALM 83:18 HCSB

There will be times when you cannot speak or defend yourself. Perhaps you are even given a chance to tell your

side of the story, but it is as if the Holy Spirit has sealed your lips. He often does this so you will be still and allow him to speak for you.

Friend, if another person is bent on accusing you for something you did not do, give God the opportunity to reveal the truth. You bear his name, and when you act in obedience to him, you can be sure he will defend you in a manner better than any you could possibly imagine.

The Lord works in amazing ways and can change the course of any human plan. Be patient and trust him, because his vindication is coming.

God, thank you for answering my prayers. Even when I wait for you to defend me, I know that you will be faithful to reveal the whole truth. Amen.

O God, do not keep silent; be not quiet,
O God, be not still.

PSALM 83:1 NIV

ENOUGH FOR TODAY

Blessed are those whose strength is in you. . . . They go from strength to strength, till each appears before God.

PSALM 84:5, 7 NIV

God has given His Word to you for several reasons. When you study it, you not only gain insight into his ways and principles, you also receive direction and encouragement.

The psalms are an excellent source of hope and comfort, especially when you are battling some intense trial.

David faced many challenges in his lifetime, but he always found the strength he needed to overcome every threat by recalling God's goodness and promises to him.

Have you learned to do the same? When trouble comes, do you turn to the Bible and ask the Lord to speak to you, or do you rush to call a friend?

The support of loved ones is essential, but the amazing love of an omnipotent God can never be replaced.

Lord, you know all things. Please help me to understand your Word and your will for me. Encourage me according to my deepest need. Amen.

*How lovely is your dwelling place, O L*ORD
Almighty! My soul yearns, even faints,
for the courts of the L*ORD; my heart and*
my flesh cry out for the living God.

PSALM **84:1–2** NIV

PEACE, IF . . .

I am listening to what the LORD God is saying;
he promises peace to us, his own people, if we
do not go back to our foolish ways.

PSALM 85:8 GNT

A deep sense of peace is yours when you turn your thoughts to God. There is always hope when you choose to listen to him instead of to the negative messages of the world.

God's Word reminds you that when you draw near to him, you will find the comfort you need. He provides the wisdom and insight to meet every challenge.

King David knew that with God's aid he could advance against a mighty army and subdue his enemies. Because of his faith, the Lord gave him many triumphs.

Not every day brings an emergency or a call for action, but many do bring a need to remember how greatly God loves you. So seek him, and receive his peace.

Thank you, dear God, for the times you express your
unconditional love toward me. Teach me your ways
so I can always abide in your peace. Amen.

God will soon save those who respect him, and his glory will be seen in our land. Love and truth belong to God's people; goodness and peace will be theirs.

PSALM 85:9–10 NCV

WHEN YOU MESS UP

*You, O Lord, are good, and ready to forgive
[our trespasses, sending them away, letting them go
completely and forever]; and You are abundant in mercy
and loving-kindness to all those who call upon You.*

PSALM 86:5 AMP

The enemy's goal is to tempt you to yield to sin. He knows
that even the smallest failure can cause guilt to rise up

within you. If he can lead you to
stumble spiritually or morally, he
can further crush you with the lie
that God wants nothing more to
do with you. Yet nothing could
be further from the truth.

The Lord hates sin because he
loves you—because sin devas-
tates your soul. However, when you confess your failings
to him and turn away from them, God embraces you with
deep affection and support.

The devil may want you to fall, but God can lift your soul.
He will never leave you.

*Teach me, Lord God, to call out to you for help and
strength rather than yield to temptation. And thank you
for forgiving me when I mess up. Amen.*

Every time I'm in trouble I call on you,
confident that you'll answer.

PSALM 86:7 MSG

ONLY ONE WILL DO

You are great and do wondrous things; you alone are God. Teach me your way, O LORD, that I may walk in your truth; unite my heart to fear your name.

PSALM 86:10–11 ESV

At times you may be tempted to think that God is not intimately aware of the dreams you have for the future.

But he is. He knows the deepest desires of your heart because he has placed many of them within you.

However, he will not compete with the desires of your heart—he wants to be your priority. If you place anything above him, he will remove it because only he deserves first place in your life.

Are the desires of your heart united to honor him? Remember that it is God who gives you life and everything you have, so honor him above all else. You may be very surprised by how he rewards your faithfulness.

God, I want you to be first in my life. Though it is painful, please remove anything that hinders me from honoring you first and foremost. Amen.

I will give thanks to you with all my heart,
O Lord my God. I will honor you forever
because your mercy toward me is great. You
have rescued me from the depths of hell.

PSALM 86:12–13 GOD'S WORD

THAT'S HIS JOB

The Most High Himself will establish her.
PSALM 87:5 AMP

Do you ever think about how much God loves you? Some people rarely take time to do this. They are burdened by their problems, stresses, and shortcomings.

They tell themselves that if they lived a better life, God would love them more. This simply is not true!

God loves you with an undivided love. Nothing you do can cause him to care for you any more or less. Rather, he accepts you just the way you are, and his ultimate goal is to build you up in his image.

God created you for a relationship with him, and he gently and compassionately molds you into all you were created to be. Therefore, rejoice! Because he is establishing you by his loving hand and will shine through you with his everlasting love.

God, I'm humbled by the fact that you love me and that you have a plan for my future. Thank you for molding me in your image. Amen.

Wonderful things are said about you.

PSALM 87:3 NCV

AVAILABLE

My eyes are weak from crying. LORD, I have prayed to you every day; I have lifted my hands in prayer to you.

PSALM 88:9 NCV

Disappointment can strike suddenly, and your first reaction may be one of defensiveness. You may feel angry and hurt; however, do not lash out. Your best course of  action is always to step away from the situation and ask God to show you what to do.

The wonderful thing about God is that he is always accessible and willing to receive you. He will show you what you need to do and comfort your aching heart.

Has discouragement assailed you? Are your eyes weak from crying and your heart tender and grieved? God will find a way to encourage you and admonish you not to give up. So turn to him—because even at this moment, he is listening for your call.

I know that when I keep my eyes on you, Lord, you will give me the comfort, the strength, and the understanding I need. Thank you for your unfailing love. Amen.

LORD, God of my salvation, I cry out before You day and night. May my prayer reach Your presence; listen to my cry.

PSALM 88:1–2 HCSB

HE KEEPS HIS PROMISES

*No, I will not break my covenant; I will
not take back a single word I said.*
PSALM 89:34 NLT

One of the deepest hurts you can experience is betrayal.
Discovering that a friend, co-worker, or loved one has

acted treacherously can tempt
you to feel defeated and
rejected. Imagine what Jesus felt
when he saw Judas walking
toward him that night in the
garden of Gethsemane.

Yet you can know that God
would never betray your trust by breaking his promises
to you. Not only would it contradict his holy character, it
would violate his perfect love for you.

Is there some precious promise that is long in being fulfilled? God has not forgotten his word to you. On the
contrary, what he is providing is too wonderful to create
quickly. Therefore, wait upon him with confidence and
hope, because he would never betray your trust.

*God, it is very difficult to wait for my dreams and hopes
to come to fruition. Yet I have confidence that you
will keep all your promises to me. Amen.*

LORD God of Hosts, who is strong like You,
LORD? Your faithfulness surrounds You.

PSALM 89:8 HCSB

FROM ETERNITY

From everlasting to everlasting, You are God. . . . For a thousand years in Your sight are like yesterday when it passes by.
PSALM 90:2, 4 NASB

There is no one like the Lord God. Nothing on this earth compares to his greatness. He can easily deal with

the ongoing operation of the universe, and at the same time be intimately interested in every detail of your day— no matter how great or small it may be.

God knew you before he formed the foundation of the earth. He is omniscient—he knows the desires of your heart and the prayers you will pray even before you lift your eyes to heaven in hopeful expectation of his answer.

As you begin your day and before you turn your light out at night, take time to thank him for caring for you so dearly and completely. His love for you is everlasting, so make sure you praise his wonderful name.

Lord, you set the heavens in place and know every star that shines. Yet you also know the slightest detail of my life and I praise you for your care. Amen.

*Teach us to number our days aright, that we may
gain a heart of wisdom. . . . Satisfy us in the
morning with your unfailing love, that we
may sing for joy and be glad all our days.*

PSALM 90:12, 14 NIV

HONEY-DO

Let the loveliness of our Lord, our God, rest on us, confirming the work that we do. Oh, yes. Affirm the work that we do!
PSALM 90:17 MSG

God may lift you up and give you a position of great responsibility. He may allow you to be like the men in

David's army, who stayed at base camp while the others rode off to fight the enemy.

Obeying him is the most important thing you will ever do. Never compare your effort to that of another. Instead, ask him to confirm you.

Are you doing what the Lord has called you to do? Do you find joy in being in the middle of His will? Can you say with confidence, "Lord, I have done my best; bless the work of my hands"?

A great sense of peace is gained by simply being what he wants you to be regardless of what this does or does not entail.

Lord God, I lift my heart up to you in praise and worship. Thank you for giving me wonderful assignments to do for your name's sake. Amen.

Let us, your servants, see your mighty deeds;
let our descendants see your glorious might.

PSALM 90:16 GNT

RESPITE FOR THE WEARY SOUL

He who dwells in the shelter of the Most High
will rest in the shadow of the Almighty.

PSALM 91:1 NIV

How does one rest in the shadow of the Almighty? The idea presented is this: You are in the presence of God no

matter where you are or what time of the day it happens to be. God is always with you, and His presence brings you an undeniable sense of peace.

This means that you can literally abide in His shelter at all times — sensing His closeness and deep affection no matter the situation. Whether you are shopping, in a business meeting, talking with a friend, or praying at home in your quiet time, he is with you.

When heartache threatens or trouble approaches, his protective cover drops down over your life, providing the spiritual comfort you need amid every storm.

God, thank you for protecting me from the troubles that
assail me. I am tired, Lord, but I am thankful that with
you I can find true rest. Amen.

He will cover you with his feathers. He will shelter you with his wings. His faithful promises are your armor and protection.

PSALM 91:4 NLT

AN ATTITUDE OF ADORATION

It is good to give thanks to the L{\small ORD}, to sing praises to your name, O Most High; to declare your steadfast love in the morning, and your faithfulness by night.
P{\small SALM} 92:1–2 {\small ESV}

Battling difficulties can be draining and may alter the way you view your circumstances. Instead of seeing the

potential of your life, you begin to feel that you are not special and that God has forgotten you. His good plan for your life seems more and more unlikely every time you think about it.

However, remember that his goal for you is always geared for ultimate victory and success. Therefore, the best remedy for your heart is to sing songs of praise to remind you of his goodness.

No matter what you are facing, God will lift your spirit when you worship him. This is what the psalmist did, which is why he wrote confidently and with great joy, "It is good to give thanks to the L{\small ORD}."

God, you are my salvation and my source of joy and gladness. Truly it is good to praise you; and no matter what happens, I'll rejoice in your love for me! Amen.

You, O LORD, have made me glad by what You have done, I will sing for joy at the works of Your hands.

PSALM 92:4 NASB

BEYOND TIME

Your throne, O LORD, has stood from time immemorial.
You yourself are from the everlasting past.

PSALM 93:2 NLT

When you acknowledge God's power and might, he pours his encouragement into your heart. A simple prayer, "Lord, I need your help," speaks volumes to him.

 He hears your confession and moves into action.

Yet there will be times when you do not have days or weeks to pray about what you are facing. An emergency will arise, and within a few minutes or even seconds, you will need His comfort and direction. Can God help you in such urgent situations?

Yes, he is perfectly able to provide all you need the moment you cry out to him.

So take heart, friend, in your faithful God. He is as faithful to you today as he has been from time immemorial. And he will surely come to your aid as soon as you call.

God, you are truly faithful—as you were yesterday, you
will be today and forevermore. Thank you that I can
always trust your mighty, loving hand. Amen.

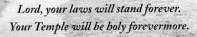

Lord, your laws will stand forever.
Your Temple will be holy forevermore.

Psalm 93:5 NCV

DISCIPLINE OF THE HEART

*How blessed the man you train, God,
the woman you instruct in your Word.*

PSALM 94:12 MSG

Have you ever considered whether you are a living reflection of God's mercy and grace to others? If not, then you

should ask God to teach you how to be an instrument of His love and understanding.

Each day you must deal with all kinds of situations—such as rude store clerks who test your patience and irate drivers in traffic who make your blood boil. However, each of these is

an opportunity for you to demonstrate your true character—to show what is really in your heart.

To react in a manner that honors God takes discipline. So the next time you are annoyed, angered, or aggravated, think of it as an opportunity to share his grace with the offender. Certainly God will bless your efforts to be more like him.

*God, there are times when I need a firm reminder that I
belong to you and my actions reflect what is hidden in my
heart. Please help me to honor you. Amen.*

When I felt my feet slipping, you came with your love and kept me steady. And when I was burdened with worries, you comforted me and made me feel secure.

PSALM 94:18–19 CEV

WHAT IS WORSHIP?

*Come, let us worship and bow down; let us kneel
before the LORD our Maker. For He is our God,
and we are the people of His pasture.*

PSALM 95:6–7 NKJV

Some people talk about being in a great house of worship
and sensing God's presence. The towering spires, stained-

glass windows, and deeply
carved wooden altar where private confessions are made are
elements that can stir your heart
with thoughts of his unconditional love, mercy, and grace.

Many times, however, the most
sacred place is found in the quietness of your own room
and in the stillness of your heart. This is where God per-
sonally meets with you, reveals himself to you through his
Word, and teaches you how to live each day with hope.

The Lord of heaven cannot be confined to a building or a
single location. He is omnipresent—everywhere at all
times. He is awesome in nature, and he is near to you now.

*God, I am in awe and wonder at your greatness. Thank
your for extending your personal love to me and for
the opportunity to live each day for you. Amen.*

Let us come before him with thanksgiving and extol him with music and song. For the LORD is the great God, the great King above all gods.

PSALM 95:2–3 NIV

NATURE DECLARES HIS PRAISE

*Let the heavens be glad and the earth rejoice;
let the sea and all that fills it resound. Let the
fields and everything in them exult.*

PSALM 96:11–12 HCSB

It is easy to think, *When I see the Lord, I'll do this or say that.* The truth is that when you see him face-to-face, the

only thing you will want to do is bow down and worship him. Words, if they are spoken, will only be those of praise and adoration. You will not be able to contain yourself or the love you feel for him. In fact, all of creation will exalt His holy name.

This is why it is so necessary to learn to praise him now. It is practice for what you will be doing for eternity. Honor him for his goodness, faithfulness, long-suffering, and provision for your every need. Sing songs of glory to his name today and every day— for surely he is worthy both now and forevermore.

God, there are times when I overlook all that you have done for me. Right now I want to thank you for taking care of all that concerns me. Amen.

The LORD is great! He should be highly praised. He should be feared more than all other gods because all the gods of the nations are idols. The LORD made the heavens.

PSALM 96:4–5 GOD'S WORD

Understanding

The fear of the LORD is the beginning of wisdom; all who follow his precepts have good understanding. To him belongs eternal praise.

PSALM 111:10 NIV

UNPREDICTABLE

Clouds and darkness are round about Him [as at Sinai];
righteousness and justice are the foundation of His throne.
PSALM 97:2 AMP

God is never surprised by the unpredictable events of
this world. He is never shaken, and he is never changed

by anything that happens. He is the
same today, tomorrow, and forever,
and he is in control of all things.

Why can you face the future with a
clear sense of hope and promise?
Because he takes care of all that concerns you. Whether the stock market
rises or falls, God remains the same.

Though health issues come and go, he will always prove
to be faithful.

You have a sure hope for your life that holds steady no
matter how stormy or bright life becomes—and that is
the hope you have in Jesus Christ.

Lord, I praise you because nothing is beyond your control.
Today if I have an unexpected challenge, please remind
me of your constant and unyielding love. Amen.

The mountains melt like wax at the presence of the LORD, at the presence of the Lord of the whole earth. The heavens declare His righteousness, and all the peoples see His glory.

PSALM 97:5–6 NKJV

HE HAS NOT FORGOTTEN

*He has remembered his steadfast love and
faithfulness to the house of Israel. All the ends
of the earth have seen the salvation of our God.*

Psalm 98:3 esv

There will be times when you wonder if God has forgotten his promises to you. He never does. Months or years

may pass, but regardless of the length of time, always remember the plans he has for you.

God does not operate according to anyone's schedule. Joseph spent years in Egyptian exile before he realized what the Lord wanted to do in his life. The time he spent in prison was not

wasted. God was preparing him for an even greater purpose and only time would reveal what this was. His responsibility was to wait obediently for the Lord to work.

This same principle applies to you. The next time you are tempted to become anxious or impatient, remember God always blesses those who are committed to waiting for and trusting him.

*God, I want to honor you with my life. Please forgive me
for pushing forward when you want me to wait, and
help me to know when you want me to advance. Amen.*

The LORD has made His victory known; He has revealed His righteousness in the sight of the nations.

PSALM 98:2 HCSB

THE IMPORTANCE OF HOLINESS

Exalt the LORD our God, and worship at
His holy hill; for the LORD our God is holy.

PSALM 99:9 NKJV

People often think that doing a certain activity will make them holy. There is only one way to begin the journey into holiness, and that is through a personal relationship with Jesus Christ.

Even though the Lord spent three years with the disciples, they still had problems that they had to overcome. Peter was impetuous; Thomas was doubtful; and the others worried whether Jesus would do what he had promised.

However, when the Holy Spirit renewed their minds, they began to respond to problems and difficulties the way Jesus had.

The closer you grow to Christ, the more you will be inspired to live a pure life.

Lord, remove everything within my life that would
prevent me from becoming like you. I love you and
want my life to honor you in every way. Amen.

Mighty King, lover of justice, you have established fairness. You have acted with justice and righteousness.

PSALM 99:4 NLT

A SONG TO SING TOGETHER

Shout praises to the LORD, everyone on this earth. Be joyful and sing as you come in to worship the LORD!

PSALM 100:1–2 CEV

Nothing in this world can bind individuals together like a vibrant faith in Jesus. In fact, the normal things that

divide people tend to melt away when they allow the abundant love of Christ to flow through them.

Believers were always meant to be unified. In fact, Revelation 7:9–10 (GNT) says that one day people from "every race, tribe, nation, and language" will together call "out in a

loud voice: 'Salvation comes from our God, who sits on the throne, and from the Lamb!'"

So next time you feel lonely or as if you don't belong, reach out to another Christian and ask what Jesus is doing in their life. Soon enough, you will find your hearts knit together in songs of praise to the Lord.

God, thank you that I have a song to sing with every other believer—a song of praise to you! Truly, you are worthy of all honor and glory! Amen.

*Realize that the L*ORD *alone is God. He made us,*
and we are his. We are his people. . . . Enter
his gates with a song of thanksgiving. Come
into his courtyards with a song of praise.
Give thanks to him; praise his name.

PSALM 100:3–4 GOD'S WORD

WHAT YOUR EYES TAKE IN

*My eyes shall be upon the faithful of the land, that
they may dwell with me; He who walks in a
blameless way is the one who will minister to me.*

PSALM 101:6 NASB

Have you ever experienced that pang of longing in your
heart that comes after an especially beautiful love story?

Or the grumbling of your stomach
after a particularly delectable
cooking demonstration? These are
small evidences of the effect that
the things you watch, read, and
listen to have on you.

Whether or not you realize it, you
are greatly influenced by the media you allow into your
life. It shapes the way you think and react to situations.
If you have been struggling in a particular area, the
shows, music, and books you have been partaking of may
have contributed to the problem.

If you think God would disapprove of something that is
influencing you—let it go.

*God, please show me if there is anything in my life that is
influencing me in a negative way. I know that you
will always keep me from harm. Amen.*

I will ponder the way that is blameless. . . . I will walk with integrity of heart within my house; I will not set before my eyes anything that is worthless.

PSALM 101:2–3 ESV

TIME IS HIS TOOL

It is time to be gracious to her,
for the appointed time has come.
PSALM 102:13 NASB

Do you ever feel as if time is your enemy? There is either too little of it when deadlines assail, or too much when

waiting for some blessed hope. Yet understand that time is not your foe. Rather, it is a precision instrument that God uses in your life to develop your potential.

Through abbreviated seasons, when there isn't enough time to get everything done, he shows you his mighty wisdom, power, and mercy. During the long years of waiting—while every emotion is tested—he molds your faith and character.

Time isn't your enemy, friend. Time is merely a tool in God's hand to reveal himself to you in a new way. His grace is sufficient for every moment of your life. So trust him and look to him *whenever* you are in need.

God, even though time is a driving factor in my life, I
thank you that I don't have to fear it. I praise you for
your lovingkindness every moment of every day. Amen.

Long ago you laid the foundation of the earth. Even the heavens are the works of your hands. They will come to an end, but . . . you remain the same, and your life will never end.

PSALM 102:25–27 GOD'S WORD

UNSURPASSED SATISFACTION

Praise the LORD, O my soul, and forget not all his
benefits . . . who satisfies your desires with good
things so that your youth is renewed like the eagle's.
PSALM 103:2, 5 NIV

A soul can only tolerate stress and self-denial for so long. When challenges or hardships consume you for a pro-

longed period of time, you must somehow quench the longings within that you've been neglecting.

At times that may mean acting out in a way that is negative—through binge eating, overspending, destructive relationships, substance abuse, or compulsive behaviors. Unfortunately, your reckless actions do nothing to fulfill you and leave you feeling more out of control and discontented than before.

Yet there is a positive way to handle your stress, and that is to spend time alone with God. He will satisfy you more than anything else ever could. He gives you exactly what you truly need.

God, help me to focus on you instead of turning to
impulsive behaviors that harm me. Only you can
truly soothe my soul and alleviate my stress. Amen.

As the heavens are high above the earth, so great are His mercy and loving-kindness toward those who reverently and worshipfully fear Him.

PSALM 103:11 AMP

FORGET IT

As far as the east is from the west, so far has
He removed our transgressions from us.
PSALM 103:12 NKJV

There may be people in your life who never allow you to
forget what you have done wrong. Every time you make

a mistake, they are quick to
pounce—reminding you of the
ways you have failed.

However, God isn't like that.
Whenever a believer repents he
says, "I'll wipe the slate clean. I'll
forget they ever sinned!" (Jeremiah 31:34 MSG).

Of course, maybe the person who is always reminding
you of your faults is . . . you.

Don't do this to yourself. God forgives you, and when he
says your sins have been erased forever, there isn't a trace
of them left in your life. Therefore, pardon yourself and
learn from your errors. Then praise him for all the grace
he has shown you.

God, thank you for forgiving all my sins and never
reminding me of the way I have failed. You are truly
loving and merciful, and I praise you! Amen.

Praise the Lord, my soul, and do not forget how kind he is. He forgives all my sins and heals all my diseases. He keeps me from the grave and blesses me with love and mercy.

PSALM 103:2–4 GNT

A MESSAGE FROM CREATION

What a wildly wonderful world, God! You made it all, with Wisdom at your side, made earth overflow with your wonderful creations.

PSALM 104:24 MSG

There will be times when your day seems far too normal. Life feels a little flat and even dull. You start your daily  routine and find yourself wondering why your attitude toward it has changed. Was there a time when it felt special, when the routine was easy and the pace of your life enjoyable?

Everyone feels this way at some point—it is as if life has lost its luster. However, there is a solution: Recall the awesome, creative power of God. The psalmist realized that when he praised God for his wondrous works, his heart lifted to new heights.

You can do the same. Discover fresh hope for your day and expectancy for the future by remembering all the awesome things God has done.

God, please draw me near to you today so that I may see you and your creation in a new way. Truly you are infinite in nature and loving in all your ways. Amen.

I will sing to the LORD as long as I live; I will sing praise to my God while I have my being. May my meditation be sweet to Him; I will be glad in the LORD.

PSALM 104:33–34 NKJV

PROVISION FROM HEAVEN

*He brought quail and satisfied them with bread
from heaven. He opened a rock, and water gushed
out; it flowed like a stream in the desert.
For He remembered His holy promise.*
PSALM 105:40–42 HCSB

Many people are tangled up in their thoughts because
they have forgotten what God has promised them in the

Bible. You do not have to follow the same path. God wants
you to understand that his
mercies are new every morning and that he will provide for
you in miraculous ways as you
travel through life.

One way he does so is through the Bible, which contains
all the hope and wisdom you need for each day. The
Bible was written for you, and the truth it contains is just
as powerful today as when it was first penned. God
promises to love, provide for, and guide you each day.

*Thank you, God, that your mercies are new every
morning and your care for me never changes. Teach me
through the Bible how to walk in your way. Amen.*

He brought Israel out with silver and gold, and no one among his tribes stumbled. . . . He spread out a cloud as a protective covering and a fire to light up the night.

PSALM 105:37, 39 GOD'S WORD

BELIEVING THE BIBLE

*He saved them for his name's sake, that he might
make known his mighty power. . . . Then they
believed his words; they sang his praise.*

PSALM 106:8, 12 ESV

Perhaps you've wondered: *What if I make the wrong
choice? What if I make a terrible mistake?* You have stayed

awake at night pondering the right
way to handle some difficult decision,
and you are fraught with anxiety.

God knows all that you are facing, and
he knows how you should handle the
situation. Will he help you with the
decision that you need to make? Will
he show you how to make the right
choice? The answer is yes, when you ask him to show
you what is best and you believe him.

He may speak to you through the Bible or through a
trusted Christian friend, but you must trust and obey
him when he speaks. Be still, listen for his answer to your
prayers, and be confident that he will lead you.

*God, I greatly admire your power. I am amazed how you
never become weary or tired of teaching me how to live
each day. I believe you, God. Lead me. Amen.*

Hallelujah! Give thanks to the LORD, for He is good; His faithful love endures forever. Who can declare the LORD's mighty acts or proclaim all the praise due Him?

PSALM 106:1–2 HCSB

OUT OF TROUBLE

They cried to the LORD in their trouble, and he saved them from their distress. He brought them out of darkness and the deepest gloom and broke away their chains.
PSALM 107:13–14 NIV

Have you ever felt like giving up? Most people have. The truth is, if you live long enough, you will battle thoughts  of discouragement, but you do not have to give in to them. There is hope even when the landscape of your life appears dark and stormy. The psalmist cried out to God, and he was saved from his distress.

What was the key to his turnaround? He acknowledged his situation to God and proclaimed his faith in God. Instead of being "me focused," he was God focused. When you are tempted to keep going, pushing to resolve a difficult issue — stop. Go to God in prayer and cry out to him. You will find that clouds of disheartenment quickly evaporate in his presence.

God, I know there are times when I have not trusted you fully, and have been discouraged because of it. Forgive me, God, and help me to have hope in you. Amen.

He sent His word and healed them,
and delivered them from their destructions.

PSALM 107:20 NASB

YOUR HAVEN IN HIM

*They were glad when it grew calm, and he
guided them to their desired haven.*

PSALM 107:30 NIV

One of the irresistible things about God is how he often gives you the desires of your heart. When your life is fully committed to him, he blesses you. This is because

the closer you are to him, the more you realize the things of the world are unworthy of your attention. Rather, you want to enjoy his pleasures.

You will also notice that the more you surrender your life to him, the more you sense his personal care for you. You experience his blessings in a new way, and may even begin to wonder what you have done to receive so much from him.

That is the way he is—God gives good things to his children. When your life is committed to him, he provides for every need you have and much more.

*God, I love to know you better—not just so I can receive
your good gifts, but also so I can truly know and enjoy
you more. You are my peaceful place of refuge. Amen.*

He hushes the storm to a calm and to a gentle whisper, so that the waves of the sea are still.

PSALM 107:29 AMP

LISTEN EXPECTANTLY

God spoke in holy splendor.
PSALM 108:7 MSG

Have you ever prayed for God to meet a need in a certain way but the answer did not come immediately. You continued to seek his will but it appeared that he was silent about the matter.

God is always at work. However, you may not see the many ways he is orchestrating the blessings he sends. How should you wait for your prayers to be answered? One of the best ways is to wait with confident expectation, knowing that he is the God of the universe and that he is intimately involved in your life.

Never be quick to jump ahead of him. Waiting with patience and with hopeful expectation of his provision is a demonstration of your faith in his ability to meet every need you have.

God, I proclaim my faith in you. You set the heavens and the earth in place, and I know you will meet every need I have with your great power and wisdom. Amen.

With God we will gain the victory.

PSALM 108:13 NIV

From All Harm

The LORD will keep you from all harm—he will watch over your life; the LORD will watch over your coming and going both now and forevermore.

PSALM 121:7–8 NIV

WOUNDS FROM A FRIEND

In return for my love, they accuse me,
but I pray for them.
PSALM 109:4 GOD'S WORD

Have you ever experienced the betrayal of a friend? What should you do when such an awful thing happens? The

psalmist turned his attention to God. He did not run to others declaring his side of the story, trying to gain support. Instead, he sought shelter in God's presence.

God is the only One who can offer the proper view of your circumstances. He helps you recall the many times you have fallen short in the same way and prepares you to forgive the person who hurt you.

Why? Because anger and resentment are unbearable weights that restrict your ability to experience his love. You can forgive those who hurt you and move on when the focus of your heart is set on the Savior.

God, please teach me how to extend grace and mercy to
those who have hurt me. Root out any bitterness,
God, and heal my wounds. Amen.

Lord, deal kindly with me for Your name's sake; because Your lovingkindness is good, deliver me; for I am afflicted and needy, and my heart is wounded within me.

PSALM 109:21–22 NASB

IN GOD'S PRESENCE

The Lord is beside you to help you.
PSALM 110:5 NCV

There is never a time when you are not with God. He is infinitely aware of your every move, thought, desire, and request. Still, one of the greatest joys you can ever experience is being in God's presence—those special moments

when he seems closer, when the answers you receive from him profoundly affect you.

In times like this, you feel as if you are sitting at God's feet, listening to his every word with a heart of intense devotion and peace.

The psalmist learned that there was joy, wisdom, and strength to be gained by drawing near to God. Have you? Have you experienced the wonder of his presence and the depth of his peace? Have you surrendered yourself to him and opened your heart to his eternal love? You should— because there is no better place to be.

God, I am listening. Help me to experience your awesome presence and mold my life into a vessel of honor that will draw others to you in a personal way. Amen.

*Your people will offer themselves willingly in the
day of Your power, in the beauty of holiness.*

PSALM 110:3 AMP

THE RIGHT STEP

*Wisdom begins with respect for the Lord; those
who obey his orders have good understanding.
He should be praised forever.*

PSALM 111:10 NCV

Have you ever longed to know what was going to happen in the future? You may be facing a problematic situation and want to make the best
choice in the matter. Or perhaps you
have been given an exciting opportunity and question whether moving
forward is the right thing to do.

God's will is not a mystery. He has a
wonderful path that he wants you to
follow, but you must be willing to do
two things: First, ask him to reveal his plan to you.
Second, be committed to obeying him even if it means
making a difficult decision.

You may be tempted to move forward without him, but
don't. Wait until you know his will, because he will certainly show you the right step to take.

*Thank you, God, for revealing your will to me when
I fully place my trust in you. You are faithful
and true, and worthy of all praise. Amen.*

All he does is just and good, and all his commandments are trustworthy. They are forever true, to be obeyed faithfully and with integrity.

PSALM 111:7–8 NLT

NOTHING TO FEAR

Good people will always be remembered. They won't be afraid of bad news; their hearts are steady because they trust the LORD. They are confident and will not be afraid.

When your life is committed to Jesus Christ, you have nothing to fear. Though you face disappointment and

hardship, the one thing that never changes is God's love for you. Difficulty comes but you can be certain that he will never fail you.

Why does the opposite seem true at times? Often because the last thing you want to do is deal with the serious problems that confront you. However, God uses adversity to prepare you for greater blessings. He stretches your faith in him—not to harm you, but to teach you to draw near to him.

Friend, your trials can either make you bitter or better. Therefore, set your heart on becoming better by drawing near to God and allowing him to work in your life.

God, I know the only way I can know you better is by allowing you to teach me what is right. Please give me the strength and courage to follow you always. Amen.

*Light arises in the darkness for the upright,
gracious, compassionate, and just.*

PSALM 112:4 AMP

FROM BARREN TO FRUITFUL

*He grants the barren woman a home, like a joyful
mother of children. Praise the LORD!*

PSALM 113:9 NKJV

Rejoice that God always provides exactly what you need.
Even if you long for children, but haven't had any, don't

fret. God has a marvelous plan
for you.

It all hinges on maintaining
the right attitude. Set a goal to
become involved in the lives of
others—especially young peo-
ple, who will remember you as a godly role model.

Years ago a young woman established a school for students who didn't have the financial ability to attend col-
lege. She believed all students should become all God
wanted them to be. Years later students continue to
remember this woman's commitment to their future.
While she never had children of her own, there is an army
of young people who saw her as a caring and godly surro-
gate mother.

*God, there are times when I doubt your purpose, especially
when it involves my desires. Give me insight into your
will so I can rejoice in all you have given me. Amen.*

He raises the poor from the dust; he lifts the needy from their misery and makes them companions of princes.

PSALM 113:7–8 GNT

THE EARTH'S TRUE MASTER

Tremble, O earth, at the presence of the Lord.
PSALM 114:7 ESV

The earth is full of the glory of God—his absolute majesty inhabits every corner. Nothing you face today can or will change this truth—no heartache, no sorrow,  and no disappointment. This may be a fallen world—one that has been tainted by sin—but soon God will return in power and might. He will restore all that has been broken.

Every created thing is subject to his command because he is the Maker and King of all that exists. So regardless of how disjointed life seems, remember he is greater than all you fear. You can rest in his presence and find all the goodness, love, mercy, gentleness, kindness, and blessing you need. The fact that the sovereign God of the universe watches over you should fill your heart with joy, hope, and peace.

God, forgive me for becoming so concerned about my problems and fearful of earthly threats. Your love is awesome; teach me to worship only You. Amen.

God brought his people out of Egypt. . . .
When the sea looked at God, it ran away,
and the Jordan River flowed upstream.

PSALM 114:1, 3 CEV

GETTING OVER YOURSELF

Not for our sake, God, no, not for our sake, but for your name's sake, show your glory. Do it on account of your merciful love, do it on account of your faithful ways.

PSALM 115:1 MSG

You may be tempted to believe your life is no more than a mundane, ordinary routine. You may do your daily tasks the same way every day, and mediocrity may characterize your tiresome existence. However, you don't have to stay in a rut.

God is creative. He wants you to grow beyond the boundaries you have set for yourself and experience the abundant life he created you for.

When you see limitations, he sees gateways to new opportunities. Trust him to use you to encourage others and to expand your narrow limits. There are many exciting opportunities for you to enjoy when you place your faith in him.

God, help me to accept new challenges so I can grow in my faith in you. Open doors so that I can become all that you want me to be. Amen.

Our God is in heaven doing whatever he wants to do. . . . May you be blessed by GOD, by GOD, who made heaven and earth.

PSALM 115:3, 15 MSG

A THANKFUL HEART

*How can I repay the LORD all
the good He has done for me?*
PSALM 116:12 HCSB

There will certainly be times when God requires you to
obey him in something that you find extremely challeng-

ing or unpleasant, and you will be
tempted to abandon what he has
called you to. This is a test of your
heart—of how you really view
your relationship with God.

Are you serving him out of a
thankful heart—willing to do
whatever he tells you to? Are you
committed to him because of

your overflowing love? Or are you trying to buy his affection through "good works"?

A difficult assignment can leave you wondering why you
should continue trusting and serving him. But when you
do, you become an authentic, living example of true praise.

*God, I want to serve you out of love and thanksgiving—not
out of obligation. Help me to offer myself wholeheartedly
no matter what you call me to do. Amen.*

GOD, here I am, your servant, your faithful servant:
set me free for your service! I'm ready to offer the
thanksgiving sacrifice and pray in the name of GOD.

PSALM 116:16–17 MSG

A PERSON HE LOVES

Great is His faithful love to us.
PSALM 117:2 HCSB

You don't need to worry about the future. God is in control and he will provide his very best for you—a daughter he loves dearly. He knows what you will face today, tomorrow, and forever, and how you  should navigate through every twist and turn that life holds. He has a wonderful plan for you, but you must accept it.

You do so by asking him to keep you in the center of his will, and trusting him as he trains you to see your life and circumstances from his loving perspective.

While problems that stretch your faith will come, you can learn to look beyond them to when God triumphantly fulfills his purpose for your life and lovingly blesses you with his great and precious promises. Truly, you will never regret trusting him.

God, teach me to be still before you and wait for your leading before I move forward. I know it is in times of quiet that you whisper truth to my heart. Amen.

Praise the LORD, all you nations!
Praise him, all you people of the world!

PSALM 117:1 GOD'S WORD

YIELDING TO TRUST

I was pushed back and about to fall,
but the LORD helped me.

PSALM 118:13 NIV

News of a sudden sorrow or a shift in the way you live life can cause you to feel shaken. You may wonder if

you'll be able to make it through another day. Frustration, stress, and pressure can overwhelm you, but you don't have to yield to discouragement. The psalmist placed his trust in God and found the help that he needed. You can too.

It may be tempting to charge ahead in your thoughts and begin to consider all that you can do to make life easier and better. However, moving forward without God's guidance will bring you even more disappointment.

The best way to proceed is to seek God's will. Listen to him and trust him to guide your every step, because you will surely enjoy his untold blessings.

God, thank you for guiding and comforting me through
every decision and distress. I acknowledge that the best
plan for my life is yours—in your timing. Amen.

The LORD is my strength and my song; he has given me victory. Songs of joy and victory are sung in the camp of the godly. The strong right arm of the LORD has done glorious things!

PSALM 118:14–15 NLT

SET ME FREE

I run in the path of your commands, for you have set my heart free. Teach me, O Lord, to follow your decrees; then I will keep them to the end.

Psalm 119:32–33 niv

Have you ever yearned to be free from your responsibilities? It isn't unusual for you to feel this way—especially

if the tasks you've been doing haven't been initiated by God. When you fail to follow God's course for your life, the activities that were once enjoyable may become burdensome obligations.

However, Jesus said, "Take my yoke upon you and learn from me, for I am gentle and humble in heart, and you will find rest for your souls. For my yoke is easy and my burden is light" (Matthew 11:29–30 niv).

Are you wearied from burdens and obligations? Then trade your yoke for his and do as he says. Surely you'll find freedom for your soul.

God, help me to keep in step with your plan by doing what you have given me to do. Strengthen me to do your will, my God, so I don't become weary. Amen.

I have gained perfect freedom by
following your teachings.

PSALM 119:45 CEV

THE SHELTER OF HIS PROMISES

Even in my suffering I was comforted
because your promise gave me life.
PSALM 119:50 GNT

When the sun is shining, it's hard to imagine the approach of a violent storm. However, a change in envi-

ronment can take place quickly. What begins as a beautiful morning may become a dark and threatening day.

However, you don't have to allow a sudden shift in climate to cause you to feel discouraged or defeated. God has vowed never to leave your side, and he is always at work on your behalf. He knows your struggles, and has promised to provide the wisdom, strength, and courage you need to stand firm in your faith.

Therefore, hide his promises and principles within your heart, so you'll have the hope you need for times of tempest. Because then, no matter how strong the winds of adversity blow, the Word of God will guide you to safety.

God, whenever pressures build and the storms of life
assail, help me to recall your wonderful promises so
that I will not be tempted to give up. Amen.

*Remember your promise to me,
your servant; it has given me hope.*

PSALM 119:49 GNT

SOMETHING TO OFFER

Those who fear You will be glad when they see me,
because I have hoped in Your word.

Psalm 119:74 NKJV

When you hear the testimony of other believers, do you ever wonder: *God, why haven't I told others what you've done for me?*

Or do you think, *My story isn't as exciting as hers. I really have nothing to offer.*

Friend, this simply isn't true.

Jesus wants you to lift him up so he can draw people to his side, and one of the ways you exalt him is by telling others what he's done for you. The very anecdote that seems so insignificant to you could be exactly what someone else needs to hear to have faith in him.

Always remember that the hope you have in Jesus Christ is like a cool drink of living water to dry and thirsty souls. So offer all you have and trust him to satisfy them.

God, there are so many things you have done for me that need to be told. Teach me to tell others about you so they will have faith in you as well. Amen.

I rejoice at Your word, as one who finds great spoil.
. . . Those who love Your law have great peace,
and nothing causes them to stumble.

PSALM 119:162, 165 NASB

DISCERNMENT

*LORD, save me from liars and
from those who plan evil.*

PSALM 120:2 NCV

Not all the blessings God sends your way are material in
nature. In fact, one of the greatest blessings he gives is a
spirit of discernment. This one gift will help you make
wise choices at every turn.

Of course, you may wonder: *How do
I gain this wonderful gift?* You begin
by spending time with God in
prayer and the study of the Bible.

The more you know about him, the
more you will understand his ways,
desires, and plans. He also will open your eyes so you're
prepared for the challenges that come your way.

When you have his discernment, you have a greater
sense of confidence and hope because you know that
God is sovereign—ready, willing, and able to reveal his
will to you and protect you in every situation.

*God, open my eyes so I can see what is right and true
according to your principles. I don't desire worldly
wisdom. I desire your truth for my life. Amen.*

In my distress I cried to the Lord,
and He answered me.

PSALM 120:1 AMP

Compassion

*Your name, O L*ORD*, endures forever; your*
*renown, O L*ORD*, throughout all ages.*
*For the L*ORD *will vindicate his people*
and have compassion on his servants.

PSALM 135:13–14 ESV

IN TIMES OF PERIL

GOD guards you from every evil, he guards your very life. He guards you when you leave and when you return, he guards you now, he guards you always.

PSALM 121:7–8 MSG

Are you facing a situation that terrifies you? Perhaps you've pondered the consequences of a misstep and the  possible pain ahead, and it's more than you can handle. The anxiety churns within you—stealing your sleep and consuming your thoughts.

Take comfort in the words of Psalm 121:7 (MSG), "GOD . . . guards your very life." You perceive no help from anywhere around you, but it's because you've failed to rely upon the One who can truly deliver you. You must look to God and trust him.

You have Someone who is fighting for you—who loves, provides for, and protects you in every circumstance of life. So have faith in him. Lift your eyes to God and realize that help is on the way.

God, you know how difficult and upsetting my situation is. Help me to trust you in and through this. Nothing is impossible for you, and so my heart will rest in your care. Amen.

I lift up my eyes to the hills. From where does my help come? My help comes from the LORD, who made heaven and earth.

PSALM 121:1–2 ESV

WORSHIPING TOGETHER

I was glad when they said to me,
"Let us go to the house of the LORD."
PSALM 122:1 NASB

Why is it important to go to church—to worship and serve God with other believers? It is important because you were created for deep fellowship with God and with his people.

Sometimes we think that "church" is merely singing a few hymns and listening to a sermon. Although that is part of it, what's missing is how you discover and implement God's purpose for your life in partnership with those who will love, encourage, and equip you. It is in relationship with other believers that God helps you become all you were created to be.

Church isn't a country club for Christians; it is a living community that exists to edify its members and glorify God. Don't avoid it! Join your brothers and sisters in Christ, and worship him together as you were created to.

God, I thank you for the church—for sisters and brothers
to share with, learn from, relate to, and depend upon.
Develop your love for the church within me. Amen.

Because of my friends and my relatives, I will pray for peace. And because of the house of the LORD our God, I will work for your good.

PSALM 122:8–9 CEV

DON'T LOSE YOUR FOCUS

Our eyes look to the LORD our God.
PSALM 123:2 ESV

Everything changes when you set your focus on God. You filter every situation through the knowledge you have of him.

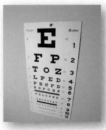

Is any problem too hard for him? No. Can he use every circumstance for your good and his glory? Yes.

Because nothing is impossible for God, every challenge you encounter is just another opportunity to see his mighty work in your life—building your confidence in him.

Unfortunately, sometimes you lose your focus. It's so easy to do—especially when trouble arises that you didn't expect. Suddenly you're wondering, *God, where are you?*

God hasn't moved; your focus has—and you must turn your attention back to him. Because he's *still* bigger than your problems and will certainly help you.

God, help me to keep my eyes on you! I praise you that nothing is ever too difficult for you and that you use everything for my good and your glory. Amen.

I lift my eyes to You, the One enthroned in heaven.
. . . Show us favor, Lord.

PSALM 123:1, 3 HCSB

THINGS COULD BE WORSE

What if the LORD had not been on our side?
PSALM 124:1 GNT

It happens without fail. Some extra money comes your way, and you know just what to do with it. Then your car breaks down. There goes your bonus. Or you finally take  a day off work, and you look forward to relaxing. Then a loved one has an emergency. There goes your vacation.

In a sense, you may feel as if you were robbed of a blessing. However, what you need to remember is that things could have been much worse. Imagine not having the money to pay for that repair, or taking that loved one to the doctor during high-pressure deadlines.

You had other plans, but God was providing for what he knew was ahead. Therefore, embrace it as a special blessing and praise him for helping you.

God, please forgive me when I have a bad attitude. Thank you so much for providing for me. I don't know what I would do without your wonderful grace! Amen.

*Blessed be God! He didn't go off and leave us. He
didn't abandon us defenseless. . . . GOD's strong name is
our help, the same GOD who made heaven and earth.*

PSALM 124:6, 8 MSG

ENCIRCLED BY STRENGTH

As the mountains surround Jerusalem, so the LORD surrounds His people from this time forth and forever.
PSALM 125:2 NKJV

The word *Jerusalem* may be translated "teaching or legacy of peace." Undoubtedly, the City of David was

very tranquil when the psalmist lived there. Buttressed by Mounts Olivet and Scopus—as well as the valleys of Hinnom, Tyropoeon, and Kidron—Jerusalem was virtually inaccessible to invading armies. She was, indeed, a place of peace.

Sadly, enemies eventually found a way in—as is generally the case with any earthly defense.

Has this happened to you? Have your earthly defenses failed you? Remember, they are imperfect and may falter, but the living God is your true protection. He will teach your heart lasting peace that none can ever take away by surrounding you with his love, wisdom, and strength from this time forth and forevermore.

God, you are and always will be my perfect Defender! I praise you for covering me with your wisdom, strength, and love. May you be exalted forever! Amen.

*Those who trust the LORD are like Mount Zion,
which can never be shaken. It remains firm forever.*

PSALM 125:1 GOD'S WORD

THE SEED OF YOUR SORROW

*Those who plant in tears will harvest with shouts
of joy. They weep as they go to plant their seed, but
they sing as they return with the harvest.*

PSALM 126:5–6 NLT

This trouble you are facing has pierced your heart and
drawn your tears. You wonder why God would allow it in

your life, especially since your rela-
tionship with him has been going so
well. However, God wants to take
you deeper. He must dig into the
tender soil of your soul.

Hebrews 12 explains, "It's the child
he loves that he disciplines. . . . At the time, discipline isn't
much fun. . . . Later, of course, it pays off handsomely, for
it's the well-trained who find themselves mature in their
relationship with God" (vv. 6, 11 MSG).

Friend, God is drawing you closer to him and growing the
priceless beauty of a godly character in you. His discipline
is difficult, but it is necessary to make you the amazing
woman he created you to be.

*God, this situation is really difficult, but I am thankful
that you have a good purpose in it and that you collect all
of my tears. Help me to trust you even more. Amen.*

Then we were filled with laughter, and we sang happy songs. . . . The LORD has done great things for us, and we are very glad.

PSALM 126:2–3 NCV

BLESSED WITH REST

*It's useless to rise early and go to bed late, and work
your worried fingers to the bone. Don't you know
he enjoys giving rest to those he loves?*

PSALM 127:2 MSG

You know all there is to accomplish and how little time
there is to finish it all; so you try to press on—straining
 your body and mind to continue.
However, it is useless. You cannot
go any further. The weariness has
completely overtaken you.

What can you do?

First, you must accept that you
need rest. Second, you must acknowledge that you're having so much trouble because you're trying to do everything
in your own strength rather than God's strength.

The task may be too big for you, but it's not too big for
him. So express your faith in him by resting in his care.
Give your burden to him, and trust him to renew you with
his energy, wisdom, and efficiency. You will be amazed at
all he will accomplish through you.

*God, it is challenging to give this burden to you, but I will
trust you with it. I rest with confidence knowing that with
your help so much more will be accomplished. Amen.*

Unless the LORD builds a house, the work of the builders is wasted. Unless the LORD protects a city, guarding it with sentries will do no good.

PSALM 127:1 NLT

THE REWARDS OF OBEDIENCE

A man who obeys the Lord will surely be blessed.
PSALM 128:4 GNT

Why not just do what you want—forgetting God's commands and following your own desires? You know the answer, because there have been times that you've done that very thing. You've gone against God's instruction

and have caused your own grief. Your plans left you unsatisfied, lonely, and full of regret.

Just the opposite has been true whenever you've submitted yourself to him. The tasks may have been difficult, but his presence energized you and you were filled with his indescribable joy. You saw his amazing work in your life and experienced the blessings of being in his will.

You know how rewarding obedience can be—so do as he says in every situation! Because "God is fair; he will not forget the work you did and the love you showed for him" (Hebrews 6:10 NCV).

God, thank you for taking note of and blessing everything I do in obedience to you. Thank you for always leading me in the best way possible. I submit myself to you. Amen.

Happy are those who respect the Lord and obey him. You will enjoy what you work for, and you will be blessed with good things.

PSALM 128:1–2 NCV

PAIN FROM THE PAST

They have afflicted me from my youth;
yet they have not prevailed against me.
PSALM 129:2 NKJV

Of the words you will never forget, how many of them are negative? The hurtful things people say and do may

stay with you a long time. Even if you've forgiven them, they affect the way you view yourself—especially if they occurred during your formative years.

God wants you to understand that he sees you as his dearly beloved daughter. He can transform your opinion of yourself through the truth of the Bible and through his tender love and heal the pain that others have caused in the past.

Don't continue to give those who hurt you power over your life. You're a child of God—a recipient of his everlasting love and salvation. Act like it. Trust him to give you the freedom from the past you yearn for.

God, thank you for setting me free from the hurtful things
others have said. Transform my understanding, and
make my life an example of your marvelous grace. Amen.

*The LORD always does right, and he has set me free
from the ropes of those cruel people.*

PSALM 129:4 CEV

IN NEED OF DELIVERANCE?

*Out of the depths I have cried to You, O LORD. . . .
There is forgiveness with You, that You may be feared.*

PSALM 130:1, 4 NASB

Are you your own worst enemy? Are you holding yourself back through your destructive behavior and negative outlook?

The truth is, you cannot escape yourself, and there are issues that you cannot solve on your own. You have wounds you do not know how to heal, sins you cannot forgive yourself for, and walls built up in your heart that you are unable to overcome by yourself.

God can deliver you from all those things. You will only remain your own worst enemy if you refuse to allow him to work in your life.

Do not make that mistake! Rather, cry out to him.

Rely on his wisdom, strength, and love.

God *can* and *will* help you.

*God, I admit that I often sabotage myself in so many
ways. Please help me. I need you and want to trust you.
Please, God, heal what I cannot. Amen.*

I wait eagerly for the LORD's help,
and in his word I trust.

PSALM 130:5 GNT

HUMBLED

My heart is not proud, O LORD. . . . I do not concern myself with great matters or things too wonderful for me. But I have stilled and quieted my soul.

PSALM 131:1–2 NIV

There's a pride problem whenever you imagine that you know better than God does. Unfortunately, it's an easy

trap to fall into. From your point of view, you know exactly how things should work out. You pray and tell God your plans and how you would like everything to fall into place.

But God says, "No" or "Wait."

Friend, you don't know better than God does because your perspective is limited. You have absolutely no idea about what's ahead or what he has in mind.

Whenever you start to believe you've got your plans all figured out—stop. Back up. Humble yourself before him and acknowledge that he is the One in control.

God, I acknowledge that I've tried to wrestle control from your omnipotent hand. Please forgive me. Teach me to humbly accept your will. Amen.

Hope in the Lord from this time forth and forever.

PSALM 131:3 AMP

YOUR HEART, HIS HOME

This is my resting place forever. Here is where I want to stay. I will bless her with plenty.
PSALM 132:14–15 NCV

When you accept Jesus as your Savior, he marks you as his own. Ephesians 4:30 (GNT) explains, "The Spirit is

God's mark of ownership on you, a guarantee that the Day will come when God will set you free." In other words, God's own Holy Spirit dwells within you—connecting you to him forever.

You cannot lose your relationship with God because it's not based on anything you can do or should refrain from. However, when you sin, you will recognize the dishonor of it because his Spirit is in your heart, saying, "Stop resisting me, beloved!"

Your heart is his home, and he works to keep you spotless, pure, and beautiful.

God, thank you that I don't need to fear losing you when I sin. Help me to live a life of holiness and hope so that your home in my heart can stay beautiful forever. Amen.

O LORD, arise, and come to your resting place.

PSALM 132:8 GOD'S WORD

AN INTERDEPENDENT PURPOSE

How good and how pleasant it is for
brethren to dwell together in unity!
PSALM 133:1 AMP

It's God's desire that harmony be a characteristic of his people. Unfortunately, sometimes the church becomes confused about how to go about achieving it. Instead of

striving for authentic unity, it settles for uniformity—a human understanding of what the church should look like. This falls short of God's will.

Rather, there is only one way to be truly unified, and that is for each person to be wholeheartedly obedient to God. God never contradicts himself, so when everyone is doing as he says, they're actually working toward the same goal, an interdependent purpose, whether they realize it or not.

Realize that the best way for you to preserve the harmony of the church is to focus your heart, soul, mind, and strength on God. He will take care of the rest.

God, I pray that my church would be devoted to serving
you wholeheartedly—so that we would have the peace,
harmony, and unity that glorify you. Amen.

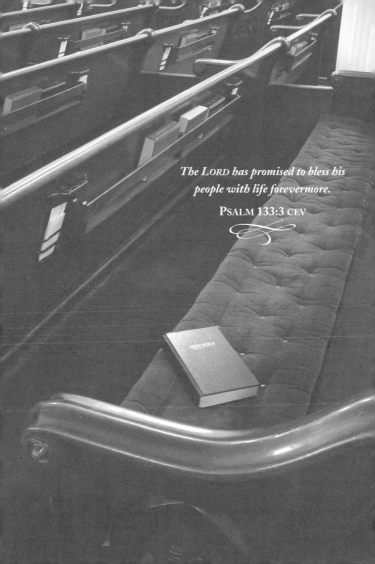

The LORD has promised to bless his people with life forevermore.

PSALM 133:3 CEV

THE SONG OF YOUR LIFE

Come, praise the LORD, all his servants.
PSALM 134:1 GNT

There are certain tunes that immediately stir your soul. The music is uplifting, the lyrics inspiring, and for some reason it touches your heart whenever you hear it.

There are some people who have the same effect on your life. A smile spreads across your face whenever you see them, and a sweet melody of faith, kindness, and joy follows them even during the most difficult times. They've set their heart on God—and it resonates to all who know them.

What does your life tell people about God? Do you inspire others to follow him?

Is your life a praise hymn—or a dirge? An overture of peace and trust—or a lament of pain and tragedy?

You can choose the tune. What will the song of your life be?

God, I want my life to be a song of worship and thanksgiving to you! Please show me how to be a person of praise. May all who meet me want to know you. Amen.

Lift up your hands to the holy place and bless the LORD!

PSALM 134:2 ESV

Praise

Let every living, breathing creature
praise God! Hallelujah!

PSALM 150:6 MSG

USELESS IDOLS

Our Lord is greater than all gods. . . . The idols of the
nations are of silver and gold, made by human hands.
They have mouths, but cannot speak, eyes, but cannot see.
PSALM 135:5, 15–16 HCSB

Anything can become an idol in your life—relationships,
activities, food, work, money, shopping, drugs—*anything.*

You know it's taken over your
heart because you'd forsake God
for the pleasure and false security
it offers. Sadly, it always leaves
you wanting more—you're unful-
filled, isolated, and it's slowly
destroying your life.

Do you find yourself heartbroken
and unsatisfied more often than not? Is there an emptiness
in you that nothing can fill? Your idol cannot help you.

God sees your needs and supplies them. He hears your
heart and provides you with understanding.

When you feel empty, turn to him and have confidence
that he will help you. He will surely fill you to overflowing.

God, please forgive me for seeking useless idols. Truly only
you can satisfy my soul in a way that gives me life and
joy. I choose you, God, and I praise you! Amen.

346

*Everyone who makes idols and all who trust
them will end up as helpless as their idols.*

PSALM 135:18 CEV

LOVE AND CREATION

The God whose skill formed the cosmos, His love never quits. The God who laid out earth on ocean foundations, His love never quits.

Have you ever considered that the creation didn't have to be so spectacular? It wasn't necessary for there to be a full  spectrum of fragrant flowers for you to admire or colorful birds to entertain you with their lovely songs. The mountains with their rugged heights, the valleys with their verdant panoramas, the briny beauty of the oceans—none of these landscapes had to exist. But they do.

Why? God created everything for you to enjoy. In this way, he reveals himself to you and expresses his love.

God always goes the extra mile to show you his love—and the creation is full evidence of this fact. So don't doubt him. He will always provide for your needs and satisfy your soul in a manner beyond all you could ask or imagine.

God, thank you for such an amazing world and for loving me so much! Help me to know your love and show you love in return. Amen.

Give thanks to the Lord of lords, for his steadfast love endures forever; to him who alone does great wonders, for his steadfast love endures forever.

PSALM 136:3–4 ESV

WHEN IT'S DIFFICULT TO PRAISE

How shall we sing the Lord's song in a strange land?
PSALM 137:4 AMP

When the inhabitants of Jerusalem were taken captive to Babylon, they lost absolutely everything. Their homes, families, and even the temple where they worshiped

God were all completely destroyed. It was as if their identity and security had been lost forever. How could they possibly praise?

Perhaps you're experiencing a similar loss—your life's been destroyed and you don't know what to do.

First, you must remember all the times God has been faithful to you in the past. Second, cling to the fact that God is still with you and is working on your behalf.

God eventually brought the people back to Jerusalem and enabled them to rebuild the temple. He will restore you as well. Look forward to that time and praise him—for he will certainly help you.

God, it is difficult, but I praise you for your past goodness to me and your faithfulness throughout history. I look forward to your deliverance and restoration. Amen.

Let my tongue stick to the roof of my mouth if I do not remember you, if I do not think about Jerusalem as my greatest joy.

PSALM 137:6 NCV

DON'T GIVE UP

The LORD will fulfill his purpose for me; your steadfast love, O LORD, endures forever.
PSALM 138:8 ESV

At times, God will allow detours to the calling and dreams you've received from him. Perhaps you experience a major setback in an important goal or relationship.  Maybe he has directed you in a way that seems counterintuitive. Whatever the case, you feel as if you are moving away from your heart's desire rather than toward it—and it is extremely disheartening.

You may be tempted to give in to your discouragement, but don't. Remember, nothing can come into your life without first passing through God's permissive hand, because he is forming you for a unique purpose.

You must express your confidence in him by patiently, steadfastly clinging to him and obeying his commands.

God, thank you for my situation—even though it is confusing to me. I will cling wholeheartedly to you and trust you to fulfill your purpose for me. Amen.

Though I walk in the midst of trouble, You will revive me; You will stretch forth Your hand . . . and Your right hand will save me.

PSALM 138:7 NASB

AN EXPERT ABOUT YOU

O LORD, you have examined me, and you know
me. . . . You are familiar with all my ways.
PSALM 139:1, 3 GOD'S WORD

No one understands you better than God—he knows you
even better than you know yourself. He has a perfect,

complete knowledge about you that is
not bound by time or human limitations. He loves you.

Whenever you begin to think that no
one appreciates the pressures you face,
remember that God does. He recog-
nizes how each trial affects you and how
each challenge molds your character.

God will not allow one area of potential in you to go
unexplored.

Have faith in your Creator and trust him to lead you to
the abundant life he formed you for. Certainly, he has
amazing blessings planned for you. Seek him first and
foremost.

God, I praise you for creating me and knowing all my life
can be. Thank you for loving me and leading me in the
very best way possible. I know I can trust you. Amen.

Search me [thoroughly], O God, and know my heart! Try me and know my thoughts! And see if there is any wicked or hurtful way in me, and lead me in the way everlasting.

PSALM 139:23–24 AMP

A BEAUTIFUL WORK OF ART

I will praise You, because I have been remarkably and wonderfully made. Your works are wonderful.
PSALM 139:14 HCSB

No matter what you think of yourself or what anyone else has ever said, the fact is that you are a masterpiece of

God. Perhaps you reject this truth because of many painful experiences. Or maybe you think that if you had a certain beauty treatment, lost some weight, or had better clothes, you would be okay.

God loves you just the way you are. When he put you together, he was delighted with the person he created.

Are you perfect? No. But you are loved by the One who is. So instead of thinking of the things that make you unique as negatives, look at them for what they really are—details that make you God's special work of art.

God, sometimes it is difficult to think of myself in a positive way. Thank you for seeing me as beautiful. Please teach me to see myself as you do—a masterpiece. Amen.

You created my inmost being. . . . Your eyes saw my unformed body. All the days ordained for me were written in your book before one of them came to be.

PSALM 139:13, 16 NIV

GUARDING YOUR ATTITUDE

O GOD the Lord, the strength of my salvation,
You have covered my head in the day of battle.

PSALM 140:7 NASB

Nothing causes a more decisive defeat than a negative attitude. When you are confronted with a challenge and

imagine it is absolutely impossible to overcome, you have already lost the battle. This will happen whenever you measure the troubles in your life against your own capabilities.

When your focus is on God's ability to help you, you have already won the victory. You cling to the fact that he protects you, provides for you, and will empower you to prevail over anything you face. This knowledge gives you the courage you need for the challenge ahead.

So guard your thoughts by covering them with God's truth. Obey him. Trust him. Never allow anything to distract you from his wonderful grace.

God, please protect me from negativity. Cover my mind
with the Bible—make it sink in and give me hope. With
you is the victory, so I will fix my thoughts on you. Amen.

Surely the righteous shall give thanks to Your name; the upright shall dwell in Your presence.

PSALM **140:13** NKJV

TROUBLESOME ATTRACTIONS

*Take away my desire to do evil or
to join others in doing wrong.*
PSALM 141:4 NCV

No one denies that temptations are truly tempting! The promise of immediate gratification will always be dangerous as long as you live on this earth.

How do you stop falling prey to the things that lure you into sin? You know Jesus has already broken the power of sin over you, but why is it still so attractive to you? How do you stop wanting the things that harm you?

Romans 12:2 (NLT) instructs, "Let God transform you into a new person by changing the way you think." Temptation begins in your thoughts; you must therefore change what you set your mind on.

Focus on God, and allow him to cleanse you with the Bible. Those troublesome temptations will not go away immediately, but over time, you will find that your desire to do wrong will certainly diminish.

*God, I know that I have often focused on the very things
that make me stumble and sin. Transform me, God,
because I want to honor you with my whole life. Amen.*

My eyes are upon You,
O GOD the Lord;
in You I take refuge.

PSALM 141:8 NKJV

ACCEPT IT AS A GIFT

A righteous person may strike me or correct me out of kindness. It is like lotion for my head. My head will not refuse it, because my prayer is directed against evil deeds.
PSALM 141:5 GOD'S WORD

When a godly person you love and respect confronts you about some fault or failure, it may sting bitterly. Perhaps

the anger rises up within you and you're tempted to defend yourself. Or perhaps you wither under her censure.

In such moments it is necessary to take a deep breath and refocus on what God is revealing to you through your loved one's words.

The truth can hurt, but if it helps you grow closer to God, then it is truly a gift that is not meant for your harm but for your good. The person who is wise, loving, honest, and courageous enough to confront you about ungodly issues in your life is a finer friend than many.

God, I thank you for my friend and for her honesty to me. God, please show me what you want me to learn from her words, and help me to respond graciously. Amen.

God, come close. . . . Treat my prayer as sweet incense rising; my raised hands are my evening prayers.

PSALM 141:1–2 MSG

ALONE

When I look beside me, I see that there is no one to help me, no one to protect me. . . . LORD, I cry to you for help; you, LORD, are my protector; you are all I want in this life.

PSALM 142:4–5 GNT

There are struggles that are so deep and hurt so badly that you cannot share them with someone else.

Uncertainty, insecurity, hurt, fear, shame, and confusion cloak your situation in darkness, hindering you from bringing the issue into the light of another's love and counsel. The loneliness of this area infects your whole life, and soon enough the feeling of alienation consumes you.

It's scary, but you must allow God to illuminate the situation so that he can set you free of the prison it has become to you. He is already working in you, so don't go through this alone. Trust him.

God, I recognize that I need your healing, but it's difficult to let go of this painful issue. Please help me. Thank you for not abandoning me in this area of need. Amen.

Set me free from my prison, that
I may praise your name. Then the
righteous will gather about me
because of your goodness to me.

PSALM 142:7 NIV

YOUR TEACHER AND COUNSELOR

Teach me to do your will, for you are my God. May your
gracious Spirit lead me forward on a firm footing.

PSALM 143:10 NLT

Sometimes following God seems more confusing than it really is. You want to be faithful to him, but other than

obeying a list of rules, you are not sure how. Isn't being a Christian more than just abiding by biblical regulations?

Of course it is! Believing in God means enjoying a wonderful relationship with him based on love. So how do you learn to please him?

Always remember that the God who is able to save you from your sins is able to teach you to live a life of love and faithfulness to him. He will patiently instruct you in how to follow him and do his will. So trust and obey him, because the Christian life is truly the most wonderful worth living.

God, thank you for teaching me how to love and serve
you! Even in this, you are guiding me faithfully. Truly
you are worthy of all honor, glory, and praise! Amen.

Teach me the way in which I should walk;
for to You I lift up my soul.

PSALM 143:8 NASB

READIED FOR WHAT'S AHEAD

*I praise you, LORD! You are my mighty rock,
and you teach me how to fight my battles.*
PSALM 144:1 CEV

It's possible that something you are facing right now has left you reeling in confusion. You've been obedient to God

and are serving him faithfully, so this new ordeal makes absolutely no sense. You are utilizing spiritual muscles that are unfamiliar and aching. Everything you believe about him is being stretched and tried in a manner you haven't experienced before.

Whether you realize it or not, you are in training. God is preparing you for important battles ahead, for the tough challenges you will face.

Do not despair! God is using this situation for your good. When you see the wonderful strengths and graces he develops in you through it, you'll surely have cause to praise him.

God, I thank you for readying me for the challenges ahead through this situation. I know you can use it for my good and your glory. Help me to trust you. Amen.

Blessed are the people whose
God is the LORD!

PSALM 144:15 ESV

THE WORD THAT ENDURES

What you have done will be praised from one generation to the next; they will proclaim your mighty acts.
PSALM 145:4 GNT

People do different things to have a lasting influence on others' lives. Many volunteer, some provide meals for

families in crisis, and others offer advice. All these things are good, but do they count for eternity? Do they have a lasting effect?

There is something you can do that God promises will endure—and that is telling others about him and directing them to the Bible.

"The rain and snow come down from the heavens and . . . water the earth. They cause the grain to grow, producing seed for the farmer and bread for the hungry. It is the same with my word. I send it out, and it always produces fruit. It will accomplish all I want it to, and it will prosper everywhere I send it" (Isaiah 55:10–11 NLT).

God, I want to have an eternal influence on this world for your name's sake. Please teach me the Bible so I can instruct others and lead them to you. Amen.

Everyone will know the mighty things you do and the glory and majesty of your kingdom. Your kingdom will go on and on, and you will rule forever. The Lord will keep all his promises.

PSALM 145:12–13 NCV

WHEN OTHERS DISAPPOINT

*Do not trust influential people, mortals who
cannot help you. When they breathe their last
breath . . . their plans come to an end.*
PSALM 146:3–4 GOD'S WORD

Don't get caught in the trap of thinking others will fulfill you or give you the joy you long for. Whether you're

hoping for someone to love, help, or honor you for some achievement, it's possible that they will let you down. That disillusion could crush your spirit.

Your first reaction may be to blame God. Understand, however, that he was not the one who disappointed you. In fact, if you had kept your eyes on him instead of that person, your heart would not be broken. Rather, you would be growing deeper in your relationship with him.

When others fail you, use it as an opportunity to refocus on God, who will always lead you in the best way possible.

*God, I acknowledge that I put too much emphasis on the
help and opinion of others. Please help me to trust you
and look only to you for help and approval. Amen.*

*The LORD sets prisoners free and heals blind eyes. He gives
a helping hand to everyone who falls. . . . He defends the
rights of orphans and widows. . . . The LORD God of
Zion will rule forever! Shout praises to the LORD!*

PSALM 146:7–10 CEV

HE PREFERS YOUR TRUST

*The Lord takes pleasure in those who reverently
and worshipfully fear Him, in those who
hope in His mercy and loving-kindness.*

PSALM 147:11 AMP

It is easy to be stuck on a certain idea of what the
Christian life should be. Going to church, reading your

Bible, having a prayer time—it
becomes a burdensome routine.
Somehow, God is left out.

However, the purpose for fellow-
shiping with other believers, study-
ing the Bible, and praying should be
so you can know him better—not so
you can check off a list of what it
means to be a "good Christian."

Be willing to give up your religious practices and pursue
a deep relationship with God. Then you won't just have
an idea of the Christian life—you'll be experiencing it
abundantly.

*God, I want to know you in an authentic, profound rela-
tionship. Teach me to have full confidence in you, my
God, for you are surely worthy of all my trust. Amen.*

How good it is to sing praises to our God, how pleasant and fitting to praise him! . . . Great is our Lord and mighty in power; his understanding has no limit.

PSALM 147:1, 5 NIV

PRAISE FROM ALL THAT EXISTS

All creation, come praise the name of the LORD.
Praise his name alone. The glory of God
is greater than heaven and earth.

PSALM 148:13 CEV

All of nature praises God, and yet sometimes it may seem unnatural to you. Why?

The creation reflects the glory of the Creator. A flower does not form its lovely petals of its own accord. The stars do not raise themselves up into the sky or shine on their own. The sea does not fill itself.

Perhaps you are far too dependent upon yourself for beauty, success, and fulfillment.

Living in dependence and praise to God is the very best, most wonderful life you could ever imagine. So open your heart to the One who created you, and discover all the beauty, success, and fulfillment he's planned for you.

God, I do praise you! Show me how to reflect your glory
and express your love so I can exalt you even better.
Certainly you are worthy of my deepest adoration. Amen.

Let every created thing give praise to the LORD, for
he issued his command, and they came into being.
He set them in place forever and ever.

PSALM 148:5–6 NLT

GOD'S DELIGHT

The Lord takes pleasure in His people; He adorns
the humble with salvation. Let the godly celebrate
in triumphal glory; let them shout for joy.
PSALM 149:4–5 HCSB

There may be times in your life when you feel as if you're
on your own—it seems that no one understands or cares

for you, and you can't do anything
right. These are the times it is
most important to remember your
Creator. God loves you, cares for
you, and works through you to
fulfill his purpose for your life.

Of course, he does not approve of
your sins, because when you com-
mit them you hurt yourself. That's why he empowers you
to turn from them and triumph over them.

Are you feeling like a failure today? Rejected, unloved,
and unworthy? Then it's time to give up your opinion of
yourself and embrace God's vision for your life.

God, in you is all my worth, glory, and joy. I thank you
for accepting and loving me. I praise you for delighting
in me and leading me to victory. Amen.

*Sing to the LORD a new song, and His praise
in the congregation of the godly ones.*

PSALM 149:1 NASB

PRAISE TO THE END

Praise the LORD! Praise God in his sanctuary; praise him in his mighty heaven! Praise him for his mighty works; praise his unequaled greatness!

PSALM 150:1–2 NLT

The book of Psalms begins: "Happy are those who . . . love the LORD's teachings" (1:1–2 NCV), and ends:

"Praise the Lord!" (150:6 NCV). In between is every situation you might experience on the journey of life—trials, losses, betrayals, joys, hopes, promises, and desires. The Psalms represent the whole spectrum of human experiences, and the faithfulness of God to walk with you through each one.

When you begin with faith in God—reading the Bible and trusting his love—you end with praise for him.

So adore him! Worship him! Express your love for him from the depths of your soul! Because he will never let you down, and surely he is worthy.

How blessed and fitting to praise you, God! May my life be a psalm of adoration to you from this time forth and forevermore. I'll love you always, my God. Amen.

Let everything that has breath praise the LORD. Praise the LORD.

PSALM 150:6 NIV